Ninety Years of the Abruzzo National Park 1922-2012: Proceedings of the Conference held in Pescasseroli, May 18-20, 2012

Edited by

Luigi Piccioni

Translated by Simona Noce and Revised by Cheryl Chapman

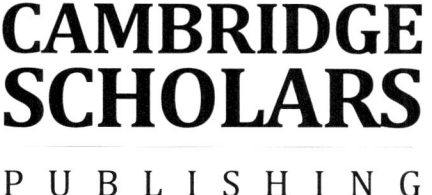

CAMBRIDGE
SCHOLARS

PUBLISHING

Ninety Years of the Abruzzo National Park 1922-2012:
Proceedings of the Conference held in Pescasseroli, May 18-20, 2012,
Edited by Luigi Piccioni

This book first published 2013

Cambridge Scholars Publishing

12 Back Chapman Street, Newcastle upon Tyne, NE6 2XX, UK

British Library Cataloguing in Publication Data
A catalogue record for this book is available from the British Library

ISBN (10): 1-4438-5058-6, ISBN (13): 978-1-4438-5058-2

TABLE OF CONTENTS

List of Illustrations vii

Preface ix
Giuseppe Rossi

Introduction 1
Luigi Piccioni

Session I: The Birth and the First Years of the National Park

The Notables of the Upper Val di Sangro and Their Role in the Genesis
of the National Park.. 5
Lorenzo Arnone Sipari

The Role of the Italian Scientific Community... 11
Franco Pedrotti

The National Park and the American Experience.......................... 25
James Sievert

Faunal Knowledge and Policies at the Origins of the National Park
and in Its First Period 31
Corradino Guacci

Session II: The National Parks of the Neighbouring Countries

The Swiss National Park and the Internationalization of Environmental
Issues at the Beginning of the XXth Century 45
François Walter

The Genesis of French National Parks 63
Henri Jaffeux

Session III: Long Term Assessments

Local Communities in the History of the Abruzzo National Park 75
Alberto D'Orazio

Environmental Law and Ethics: Autonomy or Union?
The Role of Protected Natural Areas 81
Gianluigi Ceruti

The Abruzzo National Park and the Evolution of the Protected Area
Concept in Italy 89
Carlo Alberto Graziani

The Abruzzo National Park and Nature Protection in Italy:
The Recurrences of a Centrality 103
Luigi Piccioni

Contributors 115

Illustrations 119

Index 135

LIST OF ILLUSTRATIONS

1. The upper Val di Sangro: a pastoral vocation area.
2. Since the beginnings of the twentieth century "intensive logging".
3. The royal hunt reserve: a relation between the local notables and the Crown based on the bear hunting. Hunt with the Duke of Aosta (October 1921).
4. From the royal reserve to proposal for the National Park: the first jamboree in Val Fondillo to promote the project (August 1921).
5. The 1917 first proposal for the borders of the Park.
6. The first symbol of the Park Authority, the Ente Autonomo Parco Nazionale d'Abruzzo (1923).
7. The Park Authority officers in the early 1920s (seated from left the President Erminio Sipari and the Director Nicola Tarolla).
8. The Park Rangers in the mid-1920s.
9. Touristic promotion activity: 1933 brochure in English by Park Authority-Italian railways (Ferrovie dello Stato)-National Tourist Office (Enit).
10. The symbol of the re-established Park Authority in early 1950s.
11. 1960s, a park at risk: the killing of big mammals.
12. 1960s, a park at risk: logging.
13. 1960s, a park at risk: denounce on the important national press against the construction speculation.
14. Premonitory signs of the rebirth: European Diploma of Protected Areas (1967).
15. Premonitory signs of the rebirth-international interest: Philip of Edinburgh in Pescasseroli guest of the WWF (1970).
16. The premonitory signs of the rebirth: Italia Nostra's plan for the Park (1968).
17. The new symbol of the Abruzzo National Park from the early 1970s.
18. The campaign of the mid-1970s against the ski lift on the Marsican Mountain and for the extension of the Park's borders to the endangered area.
19. Demolition of the illegal construction complex of the Cicerana, in the heart of the Park.
20. The rebirth of scientific research in the Park: "Saint Francis and the wolf" campaign (1972).

21. The launch of education activity: the enlargement and renovation of the Visitor's Centre of Pescasseroli.
22. The launch of education activity: work and study camps for young people.
23. A leading role for the movement for the Italian protected areas: the launch of the "10% Challenge" during the Camerino Conference of 1980.
24. Institutional prestige: the Minister for Environment Ripa di Meana visiting Pescasseroli in early 1990s.
25. Institutional prestige: the President of the Republic Oscar Luigi Scalfaro during his visit to Pescasseroli (1997).
26. The launch of the new millennium: the Abruzzo Lazio and Molise National Park hosts the Europarc meeting (2010).
27. An image of the conference of Pescasseroli in May 2012.

PREFACE

GIUSEPPE ROSSI
PRESIDENT OF ABRUZZO, LAZIO AND MOLISE NATIONAL PARK

Erminio Sipari, in his *Relazione alla Commissione Amministratrice dell'Ente Autonomo del Parco Nazionale d'Abruzzo del 17 maggio 1923*, on the day of his assignment as president, on November 25, 1921 said that "there was, in the presence of eminent representatives from public administrations and private institutions, a historical meeting" called by the Pro Montibus Association, "to bring about the creation of a dedicated entity intended to assume directly the task of intensifying the action to be undertaken to lead to a rapid fulfilment of the work". That is to say, the work of establishing a national park in the land of the Apennine brown bear and the Apennine chamois, which "still hide, in ever-dwindling numbers, especially in the wild area of the mountains that divide the Sangro River and the Fucino Lake, from Pescasseroli to the Valle Longa and in the dense woods around and over Opi and Civitella Alfedena".

At the November 25 meeting participated, among others, eminent exponents and representatives of cultural and touristic associations, of ministries and universities, and Sipari, who also represented the government as undersecretary of State. In this meeting

> after wide and exhaustive discussion, which was attended by all attendees, it was declared constituted, by acclamation, the Abruzzo National Park, and the Statute of the Authority was approved and a provisional Directorate of nine members was appointed with the stringent mandate to accomplish, as soon as possible, the practical organization of the Park and provide the means to guarantee its regular running.

Nevertheless, the proper inauguration of the Park took place almost a year later, a period in which there was intense cultural and political debate. It concerned the meaning of national park and the differences with the Engadine Park, created a few years earlier, where nature conservation was integral. It was decided that the Park had to be divided in two different areas: one, the genuine national park, where nature was the uncontested and protected queen; another, called *Riserva* (reserve), where socioeconomic development activities were possible and desirable, with "cultural modification, viability and habitability improvements", and, at the same time, there were special regulations for hunting and fishing, and felling and the transformation of forests were banned in order to maintain "the wise balance arranged by nature". The rules of the Park also concerned the damage of the fauna, the renting of forest and other activities. In the meanwhile, the Park Directorate resolved, on June 10, 1922, "to bring about the inauguration of the Park" on the occasion of a planned mountaineering excursion of the Crown Prince.

In the meanwhile, there was an improvement of the relationship between the Park and the Pro Montibus Association, which handed over to the Authority the acquired rights paying a regular lease, "for the amount of L. 7,500 per year", not only to the Opi village council for the first 500 hectares in the Val Fondillo "the green and most precious gem of the Park", but also to the villages of Civitella Alfedena, Pescasseroli, Villavallelonga, Lecce nei Marsi, Gioia dei Marsi and Bisegna, which made available other marvellously beautiful and interesting lands" for an overall surface of 12,000 hectares.

To obtain this result, it took many and patient negotiations to overcome "inveterate prejudices and subdue multiform interests safeguarded with desperate obstinacy". The adoption of more than fifteen resolutions by the affected village councils were necessary and those who "know the life, the tantrums and the rivalries of small mountain villages" can imagine how many and which difficulties were overcome, to succeed in convincing the local administrations and councils about the effectiveness and usefulness to be derived from the creation of the protected area, not just for the payment of a fixed annual rent, but also for the opportunity offered to those places to develop the first touristic activities. In this direction went the multi-year administration and management program developed by Erminio Sipari, whose main points were the building and the improvement of touristic accommodation facilities, also with grants for the construction of refuges and small hotels, the development of "advertising", the improvement of the road network and reforestation.

Thus the Park was solemnly inaugurated on September 9, 1922 in the presence of the political, governmental, cultural, religious and local authorities and all mayors and secretaries of the villages of the Park. There were also ministers, undersecretaries, members of Parliament, scholars, and academics. The ceremony is recorded by an inscription where it took place, near the fountain of Saint Rocco "at the first houses of Pescasseroli, toward Gioia": "The Abruzzo National Park established for the protection of sylvan beauties and nature's treasures here inaugurated on IX Sept. MCMXXII". This solemn ceremony, Erminio Sipari writes,

> had great echo in the main daily press, which wrote about it with great sympathy and deep enthusiasm, attracting the interest of Italian and foreign public opinion towards the brilliant initiative.

At the end of this "constituent" path, there was the Royal Legislative Decree no. 257/1923 of January 11, converted into Law no. 1511/1923 of July 12.

In reconstructing the event of the Park's creation, we have to remember that the idea emerged at the beginning of the previous decade, thanks to eminent naturalists, including the zoologist Alessandro Ghigi and the botanist Romualdo Pirotta, and developed in the proposal, made in 1917, of an ambitious project for a protected land in the Central Apennines, 173.000 hectares wide. The proposal of conservation of such a large area was accompanied by a thorough map with the habitats of the two most important and precious species to protect.

Nevertheless, the history of the Park could be dated back even to 1860, the Italian unification, and to the constitution of the first national park in the world, the Yellowstone National Park, in 1872. It was actually in 1860, when Leonardo Dorotea, mayor of Villetta Barrea, launching the idea of the creation of a royal hunting reserve exposed to the village council its purposes and utility, referring to the fauna and the re-introduction of some extinct species, the agro-sylvo-pastoral heritage, tourism, and public service facilities. In this simple proposal it is possible to see the way that it would develop in the following years, leading to the birth of the Abruzzo National Park. In 1872 the hunting reserve was established and, with alternate events–abolitions and rehabilitation–reached 1913, when the idea of establishing a national park, based on the proposal of 1907, really began to take shape.

In that period, following the example of the United States and Germany, also in Switzerland there was the proposal of the establishment of national parks. In 1909 was constituted the Ligue Suisse pour la Protection de la Nature, which leased, in the following years, lands in Zernez and other villages, passing then the contracts from the League to the Swiss Confederation. In the meanwhile, also in Italy associations for the "Italian picturesque and natural" monuments were founded. Thus the idea of the Abruzzo National Park was born.

The first years of the park were distinguished by some territorial enlargement, important promotional initiatives, and considerable financial, administrative and political difficulties.

In 1923 the Park had 18,000 hectares. The following enlargement in 1925 and 1926 brought it to 30,000 hectares and remained so until 1976 when, after the historic extension to the Marsicano and Godi mountains and cruel struggles in the environmentalist world and in part, also local, of the most open-minded and farsighted political-administrative world, the Park gained another 10,000 hectares. Then, in 1990 arrived other measures for the Mainarde and in 1999 for the Giovenco Valley, which brought the Park to the present size of 50,000 hectares and a buffer zone of external protection (the *area contigua*, the adjoining area) of 130,000 hectares.

In 1933 the Authority was abolished and until 1950, when it was built up again, the efforts for nature conservation and the promotional and management activities regressed considerably. In 1951, on the impulse of a renewed institutional commitment, the Park began working normally, up to the 1960s, when deep local changes and brutal speculative aggressions put its existence seriously in danger.

From 1969, thanks to pivotal battles to defend the Park, marked by press campaigns, national and international motions, continuous demonstrations in support of it, and a renewed Directorate of the Authority, the revival of the Park began and the debate on nature conservation regained strength all over Italy, a debate that finally would lead to the approval of the 1991 framework law. The Abruzzo National Park, today the Abruzzo, Lazio and Molise National Park (the law n. 93/2001 of March 29 changed the name), surely was, and in many ways still is, an important, sometimes almost exclusive, landmark of nature conservation in Italy, representing also one of the constituent elements of Italy's image abroad.

Thinking of the Park, we know we can refer to a land of extraordinary beauty, keeper of an incomparable natural and biodiversity heritage; to an innovative and farsighted commitment of citizens, institutions and the scientific community expressed, on a general level, in various circumstances and during years of intense activity, scientific and cultural debates, and controversies on conservation and local development: from 1922, when, in the overview of the European protected areas, after the first national parks in Sweden, Switzerland, and Spain, exclusive kingdoms of nature, a special park was born. A park rich in magnificent and luxuriant woods, rare animal species, including the majestic and fascinating Marsican brown bear and the Abruzzo chamois, and many other naturalistic preciousness, but that also represented a peculiar and unique entity, hosting in its territory so much human culture.

In recent years, as a kind of repetition of the history of the past decades, the life of the Park has been especially hard and difficult. And it still is. But today the Park, gradually overcoming difficulties, thinking about the future and conscious of its role in the context of Italian, European and global protected areas, works on the basis of modern principles of conservation, of an aware local promotion, participation, and dialogue.

Entering its territory we can perceive the clear sensation of being in a different place, a place where *nature is protected*, where nature deserves a special respect and has to be free to develop spontaneously. But that is not all. It is a place where villages, perched on the slopes of the mountains, show to the visitor all their architectural beauty, the result of a long generative process that has defined their social and cultural identity, whose traces are in the activities and in the material and spiritual productions of the inhabitants.

But, as we said, the Park is mainly the reign of nature, the "natural heart of the Apennine". The beech forests cover more than 60% of the land; woods of Turkey oak, maples, yews, European black pine and rare formations of birches alternate in the landscape softening the rocky peaks and the cliffs of the wildest zones. The fauna is the richest of Western Europe. The Abruzzo chamois, present with hundreds of specimens, is one of the most beautiful and rare animals of the world. However, the most fascinating presence is the Marsican brown bear. Unfortunately, very few specimens remain of this big, shy and pacific mammal (a survivor from the last glacial era, in this last strip of intact nature of the Apennine), a fact which renders it even more frail and precious. The risk of extinction is serious and the commitment of institutions to save it should be determined. In the quietest areas, it is easy to perceive the presence of the Italian wolf, the deer and roe deer, the hare, the European badger and many other animals.

The fauna of the sky is rich in fascinating protagonists such as the golden eagle, the sparrow hawk, the Common raven, the Eurasian eagle-owl, the white-backed woodpecker and many birds which have found their reign in the woods, along the streams and on the lake shores. In the undergrowth the rarest specimens of the gorgeous Lady's-slipper orchid bloom, while the beds of creeks and rivers host salamanders, yellow-bellied toads, white-clawed crayfishes and brown trout. On the bright mountain cliffs, among yellow and white wood anemones and beautiful formations of junipers and mountain pines, live the rare *vipera ursinii* and small groups of rock partridge, hidden among the rocks, the wall creeper, the Alpine accentor, the peregrine falcon, the common rock thrush, and the Alpine and red-billed choughs.

Well, the Park works and will work to preserve all this, because its main purpose is to protect nature, but it works and will work also to achieve the best integration between human beings and environment, safeguarding the anthropological, historical, archaeological and architectural values and the compatible productive activities.

An integral part of this commitment of safeguarding regards the exploitation of the historical memory, as of the institutional events and activities of the Park as well as the social, political and cultural events of the territory. The publication of the proceedings of the Pescasseroli conference held in May 2012 for the ninety years of the reserve's institution represents a conscious effort towards the construction of a shared memory, to which the Park Authority intends to further contribute with passion and energy.

Thus it is with great honour and special delight that I present here these proceedings.

Obviously, I do this not just because I personally followed the development of the organisation and the course of this important opportunity for meeting and discussion, for which great credit goes to the efforts of Luigi Piccioni and the staff of employees and collaborators of the Authority, but also because I experience this event with real, even "personal" emotion. Especially because I have lived many of these ninety years of the Park's life. As a child, here, in these places, then as a boy, then as a man, I have worked in this territory and for the Authority for many years.

From Sipari's first intuition till now, many things have changed. Probably, more than anything the reasons for which we continue to support an organisation and an institution like our National Park have changed. Even if today's objectives may look like those of ninety years ago, that is the protection of an absolutely unique fauna and ecosystem in the Italian and European local and naturalistic overview, the historical context, however, makes thoroughly peculiar and different these intentions today. Furthermore, the public and general awareness of Italian people towards the subject and the issues relating to nature and biodiversity preservation has also deeply changed. In ninety years Italy has changed deeply, its social and economic, therefore also its territorial structure has changed. The Italian land was intensely exploited, used with more or less intelligence and honesty from the economic, rational, efficient point of view: there have been many wrong, inefficient, short-sighted choices and much waste. Surely the choice of the Abruzzo National Park–the protection of a place of unique naturalistic value–was strategically important. But today, if we can imagine, it is even more important. It is so because places like this in Italy and Europe are getting rarer, more difficult to find and understand. But, perhaps, by virtue of this rarity, they are also easier places to love, from which to capture, I would say, the ethical as well as the economic, social and cultural value.

In 2012, the challenges for Italian biodiversity protection are more complex than ever. Still today, after ninety years of varying degrees of strictness, intensity and management activities, the issues and objectives that started the Abruzzo National Park experience in 1922 remain more or less the same, because the species and the habitats, which at the beginning of the 1920s started to be protected, are still endangered or at risk of degradation. While in the 1920s the danger came mainly from excessive hunting and practices of killing of the wild fauna extremely widespread even among the local populations, today the same danger comes from an excessive exploitation of the land, a diffused anthropic pressure, a pervasive fragmentation of the ecological and naturalistic homogeneity and continuity of the Park's habitats. This harms the territory. Wounds that maintain a certain level of danger for the protection of some very important species, first of all the Marsican brown bear.

Now, thus, on the occasion of this historical congress, the dialogue and the important debate among Italian and international colleagues, even friends of a lifetime, as well as among young scholars and technicians, which through these proceedings can be traced by readers, represent a fundamental and important opportunity to take stock of the challenges that have involved the Park in these decades and will continue to involve it. Some challenges have been taken on and won, others have been taken on and maybe lost; some challenges have not been adequately pursued and it is definitely the moment to face them. Certainly new challenges have emerged; interesting paths that an integrated management of the Park, both by the Authority and the other institutions involved will build up and pursue.

The management of this land, thanks also to an event like this and to the considerations and the evidence reported in these proceedings can begin to work out, we hope, a new, fundamental idea of rational planning, a complex and rich general idea on how to give coherence and impulse to local activities in a project that is linked to the key objective of nature and landscape preservation.

It is a necessary foresight, whose base is the indispensable dialogue between institutions and citizens: it is this element, for instance, that we have tried to best emphasise in the most recent years. Because without dialogue, without debate, it is impossible to design an effective plan, able to give results on the land. From my point of view, I think that a lack of dialogue and debate would have the effect of reducing the most institutional needs of a protected area, needs with national and international impacts like the preservation and valorisation of a naturalistic heritage of huge importance on a European level, which the Park is called to pursue as its first requests.

This was also, from a historical point of view, the peculiarity of the pilot project of the Abruzzo National Park, the involvement of various institutions and the resident populations in the management and local strategic choices. But today perhaps this synergy is not yet sufficiently developed: it will have to increase, improve, especially culturally, because these lands have the opportunity to preserve and offer to the community an extraordinary heritage of international interest. Only in this way, with an opening to the world, working together, improving mutually, we might safeguard definitively our land and its biodiversity, which is the main aim of the Park.

Special thanks go to all the authors of the important speeches and contributions of the conference, and thus of these proceedings, hoping that they are a chance for useful considerations to be followed by brilliant operative choices.

Introduction

Luigi Piccioni

To celebrate its ninetieth anniversary, the Authority of the National Park of Abruzzo, Lazio and Molise organised a calendar of events in which the historical dimension took on a leading role.

In these terms the international meeting at Pescasseroli from May 18 to 20, 2012, whose proceedings are published here, undoubtedly formed a major part.

Some fundamental principles were followed whilst planning and carrying out that meeting. First and foremost, to avoid the eventual contamination of excessively contingent worries, namely, to avert common topical matters, whether political or administrative, the choice was made to concentrate on re-construction and historiographical balance.

The two elements which mainly characterised the meeting evolved from this basic platform: on the one hand, the choice of scholars who have been important witnesses or of witnesses with a high degree of expertise concerning the past; on the other hand, its tripartite structure.

In fact, this meeting began with a session dedicated to its birth, that is, the re-construction of the various aspects of the genesis and first years of the Park's existence, entrusted to four scholars who, during the last 25 years, have made an indelible mark on the studies of this topic: Lorenzo Arnone Sipari, Corradino Guacci, Franco Pedrotti and James Sievert.

In comparison, the second session aimed at underlining two of the most important features of the Park's life, namely, its size and its international fame, inviting two names of prestige to contribute: Henri Jaffeux, a French high official who has devoted his long and prolific ministerial career to protected areas and who now writes about and promotes environmental history, and the Swiss François Walter, one of the major specialists worldwide on the history of conservation cultures.

Finally, the third session's target was to weigh up the entire parable of the Park's ninety years of existence, analysing its contribution to nature protection in Italy (Piccioni) and to the concept of protected areas (Graziani), the changeable relations between population and Park

(D'Orazio) and the connections between environmental rights and ethics (Ceruti).

From the speakers' analyses and the various testimonies that took place, the constant centrality of the Abruzzo reserve became more and more evident, in its stages of splendour as well as its moments of drama, in both its Italian and its international contexts. It is to be hoped that the wealth of the meeting at Pescasseroli may consolidate and strengthen an unabated authoritativeness.

SESSION I:

THE BIRTH AND THE FIRST YEARS
OF THE NATIONAL PARK

THE NOTABLES OF THE UPPER VAL DI SANGRO AND THEIR ROLE IN THE GENESIS OF THE NATIONAL PARK

LORENZO ARNONE SIPARI

The debate on the possible ways of nature conservation developed in Italy during the first two decades of the twentieth century was contained in the Law n. 778/1922 of June 11 "For the protection of natural beauty and properties representing a notable historical interest". This normative provision that was also set as legal basis for the institution of the first protected areas largely drew on the bill introduced in the Senate, during the session of September 25, 1920, by Benedetto Croce as minister of Public Education. Croce, it should be noted, who in that period expressed the need to gather in a precise legislative framework the requests of the first composite movement for nature conservation, was studying the descending curve of his maternal ancestors, the Siparis, as an example of that new bourgeoisie that, during the nineteenth century, replaced, for wealth and social authority, the ancien régime lineages. The reference, obviously, is the monograph of Pescasseroli published by Laterza in February 1922, included, three years later, as is well-known, together with that of Monterodomo, in the appendix of *Storia del Regno di Napoli*. The study of the native town of the philosopher, apart from the Crocian methodology involved to pinpoint in the historical outlines of a village the salient features of the more general history, fell expressly within an articulate series of propaganda activities in favour of establishing the Abruzzo National Park in the making.

It is not a coincidence that the upper Val di Sangro at the end of the Liberal Age witnessed a succession of initiatives of similar kind, useful to make known the peculiar natural and landscape beauty of the land outside the Apennine microcosm, through articles and photographic reports, which were published in many reviews both popular and scientific. In little more than one year, between the summer of 1921 and the autumn of 1922, the land of Abruzzo registered the organization of a national boy scout jamboree with more than six hundred young people (August 1921) and a

Marsican brown bear hunt with the participation of Prince Amedeo, Duke of Apulia (October 1921), besides, the first case in Italy, the establishment of a Park Authority, the Abruzzo National Park Authority (November 25, 1921), and the following inauguration of the protected area (September 9, 1922), in a ceremony where, to strengthen–if possible–the solemnity, the Great War memorial to the dead soldiers from Pescasseroli was unveiled. In the same circumstances, there was the establishment of the Condotta forestale marsicana (Marsican Forest Office) (October 1922), the first consortium of this sort in the Peninsula which preceded the mounting of a camp for the stay of over one hundred members of the Italian Touring Club. These events, alternated without continuous progress, soon before and after the establishment of the Park, and arranged with these purposes, sealed the fulfilment of a course begun, as we can see, more than fifty years earlier.

Thus, the cultural and local roots of the protected area of the upper Val di Sangro lay in the institution of a royal hunting reserve. Such an exclusive privilege had been proposed many times, between 1860 and 1861, by Doctor Leonardo Dorotea from Villetta Barrea. He was keen on hunting and published a "zoological compendium" entitled *Della caccia e della pesca nel Caraceno* which gave an accurate description of some of the main native animal species, whose presence, in the author's opinion, guaranteed a local reserve to compete with the appeal and the charm of similar although older and more famous institutions. Moreover, only in Central-Southern Italy belonging to the former Kingdom of Naples were there more than twenty open and active places for the exclusive hunting of the royal family members. Dorotea's efforts–launched by the municipal administration and aimed to unseat the anonymity of the area–collided with more or less insurmountable matters that hindered their realization.

A decade later, the program of the intellectual from Villetta, who in the meanwhile had died, was resumed by the two brothers Carmelo and Francesco Saverio Sipari, representatives of the sheep-owning bourgeoisie from Pescasseroli. Like Dorotea, they were hunters; however, to achieve the aim they used a different mean, which is private enterprise, donating to Vittorio Emanuele II, in June of 1872, the hunting rights over about 600 hectares, mainly high-mountain pastures, of which they were owners in the Villavallelonga village.

It stands to reason that that re-use of the pastures, with the change of function, in other words the exclusive bear hunting rights, had been suggested, at least in those families historically tied to the Apennine transhumance, by the definitive freeing of the Tavoliere (1865), which caused a considerable reduction of sheep stock. From that, the need for diversifying interests, investing somewhere else in different economical and productive sectors, and, for those who had greater flexibility and dynamism, also towards symbolic choices. One of these was the so-called "gift of the bear" that represented the instance of the upper Val di Sangro. The gift of the most sought-after and mysterious wild beast in Europe met the logic of the present as a vehicle susceptible, in a possible but not owed reciprocity, of both social rising for the individual and benefits for the land. While the individual might gain the Royal House's important gratitude, the designation to one of the various degrees of knighthood, or the opportunity of entering élite circles, on the other hand, for the land the presence of the king and his entourage could guarantee, as it actually did, a favourable repercussion in terms of repopulation of animal species, construction, road system improvement, and a more accurate monitoring, especially of the woodland heritage.

As a matter of fact, the King accepted the above mentioned gift and a few months later the act of the Sipari brothers was emulated by the villages of Opi, Pescasseroli, Lecce nei Marsi, Gioia dei Marsi, Villavallelonga, Collelongo, Balsorano, and Castellafiume and on their land was established the first royal reserve in the upper Val di Sangro. It functioned until the beginning of 1878, when it was abolished after the accession of Umberto I, who was not keen on hunting. The local notables did not remain indifferent to such a loss, but, notwithstanding the controversies and the efforts of deferring the new king, they had to wait for more than two decades before another similar exclusive privilege would be realized again.

In this respect, the foundations were laid in 1899. In the autumn of that year, Carmelo Sipari, with the support of the Member of Parliament Mansueto De Amicis, organised a bear hunt with the participation of the Prince of Naples, who, shortly afterwards, as we know, would succeed to the throne of Italy with the name of Vittorio Emanuele III. The emotions offered by the landscape and the enchanting events of the hunt, whose purpose was to hunt a rare animal like the Marsican plantigrade, and the warm but attentive hospitality received in Pescasseroli persuaded the King to boost decisively the establishment of a second hunting reserve. As a matter of fact, it was promptly ratified in the early nineteenth century, affecting the area of eleven municipalities: Alfedena, Barrea, Civitella, Villetta, and Pizzone were part of it, while Balsorano and Castellafiume did not repeat the experience. It functioned until the end of 1912, relentlessly undermined by the increasing costs to compensate for the damages of the wild fauna. It is established opinion, however, that the two institutions represented an example of a pioneering protected area. About this, it is enough to indicate that, apart from their form of exclusive privilege, the even meagre sources survey the killing of eight bears in the over-all twenty years of existence, against the twenty-seven and twelve killings attested in the year after 1878 and in the two-year period 1913-14, respectively. It should not be overlooked, furthermore, that if, on the one hand, with the second of the two reserves, the features of the future Abruzzo National Park were outlined, thanks to private enterprise, that is the strategies planned by the notable; on the other hand, the full support given by the municipal administration and the populations allowed these peculiar exclusive privileges to insert themselves completely in the local social and economic fabric, moreover, contributing to reinforce it. Ultimately, it should be noted that before the last and definitive abolition of the reserve an attention to the promotion of the land had emerged. Erminio Sipari, creator and first president of the Abruzzo National Park, was the interpreter of this interest. Erminio, son and nephew of the above mentioned Carmelo and Francesco Saverio, respectively, and also cousin of Croce, who would dedicate to him the monograph of Pescasseroli, characterised his life for a continuing dialogue with the main European cultural and technological requests. With a degree in Engineering, discipline in which he specialized abroad, and member of Parliament of the Kingdom of Italy from 1913 to 1929, since 1909 he had advocated the construction of a hotel in the main town of the upper Val di Sangro district, anticipating its future as a health resort.

At the same time, he made friends and relatives aware of the need to spread abroad the beauty of the land, especially promoting press campaigns and focused publications. An example of the latter is Emidio Agostinone's volume *Altipiani d'Abruzzo*, published in 1912 in the prestigious collection "Italia Artistica" edited by Corrado Ricci. This work, enhanced by 206 illustrations, of which almost one fourth dedicated to the future protected land, presented for the first time the effective motto "*e l'orso c'è*" (and there is the bear) that would be found in some articles in the 1920s ratifying the change from a vision of the bear as prey to another in which the plantigrade was erected as a symbol of naturalistic protection.

However, in both visions, the gift of the bear was intended as a useful means to promote the image of the upper Val di Sangro. This lets us affirm that, at least a decade earlier than 1922, following the above-outlined path, that model that was in embryo, harmoniously weaving together nature protection and touristic development, would characterise the establishment and the development of the Abruzzo National Park. Thus, at its beginnings, it was crucial and on some occasions pioneering the role played by the local notables who were able to perceive the opportunities of social and economic growth of the land, channelling them towards "sustainable" achievements.

Bibliography

Agostinone, Emidio. 1912. *Altipiani d'Abruzzo*. Bergamo: Istituto italiano d'arti grafiche.

Arnone Sipari, Lorenzo. 1998. Dalla Riserva Reale dell'Alta Val di Sangro alla costituzione del Parco Nazionale d'Abruzzo. In Emiliano Giancristofaro (ed.), *La lunga guerra per il Parco Nazionale d'Abruzzo*. 49-66. Lanciano: Rivista Abruzzese.

—. 2003. Il percorso di Croce all'ecologia liberale attraverso le radici materne. In Lorenzo Arnone Sipari, Annalisa Sorrentino, Giuseppe Varone (eds.), *Croce tra noi*. Atripalda: Mephite.

—. 2011. Introduzione. In Lorenzo Arnone Sipari (ed.), *Scritti scelti di Erminio Sipari sul Parco Nazionale d'Abruzzo (1922-1933)*, 11-41. Trento, Temi.

Croce, Benedetto. 1922. *Pescasseroli*. Bari: Laterza.

Piccioni, Luigi. 1996. "Il dono dell'orso". Abitanti e plantigradi dell'Alta Val di Sangro tra Otto e Novecento. *Abruzzo contemporaneo* s. II n. 2: 61-113.

—. 1997. *Erminio Sipari. Origini sociali e opere dell'artefice del Parco Nazionale d'Abruzzo*, Camerino: Università degli Studi di Camerino.

Sievert, James. 2000. *The Origins of Nature Conservation in Italy*. Bern: Lang.

Sipari, Erminio. 1926. *Relazione del Presidente del Direttorio provvisorio dell'Ente Autonomo del Parco Nazionale d'Abruzzo alla Commissione Amministratrice dell'Ente stesso, nominata con Regio Decreto 25 marzo 1923*. Tivoli: Maiella.

THE ROLE OF THE ITALIAN SCIENTIFIC COMMUNITY

FRANCO PEDROTTI

At the beginning of the 1900s the subject of national parks was already set out due to the first Italian nature conservation organisations such as the Associazione nazionale per i paesaggi e per i monumenti pittoreschi d'Italia (National Association for Picturesque Landscapes and Monuments of Italy), the Lega nazionale per la protezione dei monumenti naturali (National League for the Protection of Natural Monuments), and the Società Pro Montibus et Sylvis (Association for Mountains and Forests), flanked by two scientific associations, the Società Botanica Italiana (Italian Botanical Society) and the Unione Zoologica Italiana (Italian Zoological Union). They were all animated by some enlightened pioneers, as is well and widely documented in Luigi Piccioni's work *Il volto amato della patria. Il primo movimento per la protezione della natura in Italia 1880-1934.*

There were many parks to think about, but two of them had, from the first moment, a particular importance: the Gran Paradiso and the Abruzzo Parks; both have a common history, because they have the same beginnings, originating from pre-existent royal hunting reserves, even if the paths for their effective establishment were different.

It is not a coincidence that both in Val d'Aosta and in the Sangro Valley–even if in different historical backgrounds–the naturalistic tradition is great due to the presence of a fauna which had disappeared in other places and to the royal hunting reserves; it is not a coincidence that in these valleys was born a widespread conservation culture not only among important local figures, but also in a part of the population.

From the Sangro Valley came Francesco Saverio and Carmelo Sipari from Pescasseroli, Leonardo Dorotea from Villetta Barrea, Alessandro Ursitti from Opi, Giovanni Di Pirro from Pescasseroli, Nestore and Nicola Tarolla from Civitella Alfedena; from the Comino Valley came Erminio Sipari of Alvito (but he was a native of Pescasseroli) and from the Marsica

Loreto Grande of Villavallelonga, all of them involved in nature conservation and Abruzzo National Park issues.

The two parks of Abruzzo and Gran Paradiso were born in the same period; in the 1930s the respective authorities were dissolved and taken over by the Milizia forestale (Forestry Militia); both were born again with great efforts in the post-war period and made huge progress in nature protection, but they also had to suffer environmental outrages with a heavy impact on the environment.

They represent a classic reference model for the national parks established in Italy in later years.

The land (geographic knowledge)

The reference land for the establishment of a national park in Abruzzo includes the Marsica, the upper Val di Sangro, the Sagittario Valley, the Cinque Miglia and Quarto di Santa Chiara plateaux, the Comino Valley, and the group of the Mainarde.

It is an immense land, well-defined on the map enclosed in Professor Pietro Romualdo Pirotta's 1917 proposal, extraordinarily appealing from the environmental point of view and of great scientific interest, but big, too big to establish a national park in Italy's economic and social conditions of that time. In effect, the park was necessarily founded in a smaller area than that originally proposed by Pirotta.

This land had already been the subject of publications that illustrated the over-all geographic characteristics and the landscape attractions; it is enough to cite Agostinone's volume *Altipiani d'Abruzzo* of 1912. But, altogether, it was a quite isolated area, difficult to reach, almost unknown to the general public.

In all its valleys and plateaux there are towns rich in history and culture, built in the typical style of the Abruzzo architecture, with churches and palaces which are often real works of art: in the Marsica Villavallelonga, Collelongo, Gioia nei Marsi, and Lecce nei Marsi; in the upper Val di Sangro, Gioia Vecchia, Pescasseroli, Opi, Villetta Barrea, Civitella Alfedena, Barrea, and, lower, Alfedena, Scontrone, and Castel di Sangro; in the Sagittario Valley, Scanno and Anversa; on the Cinque Miglia and Quarto di Santa Chiara plateaux, Roccaraso, Pescostanzo, and Rivisondoli; on the Lazio side, Alvito, San Donato Val di Comino, Settefrati, Picinisco, and S. Biagio Saracinisco; on the slopes of the group of the Mainarde in Molise, Pizzone, Castelnuovo a Volturno, Rocchetta a Volturno, etc. Many books have been dedicated to these places, describing their history, art, personalities, and architecture; some of them are cited in the enclosed bibliography.

The life of these towns was exclusively based on agro-sylvan-pastoral activities: mountain farming, forestry, and sheep farming. The long transhumance routes climbed down from Abruzzo to the Tavoliere of Foggia, in the middle of which there is a small residuary wood on the Cervaro river, called the Bosco dell'Incoronata. Pescasseroli was like the terminus of the shepherd's track that came up from Puglia and at its two extremities there are two churches, both dedicated to the Madonna dell'Incoronata (Our Crowned Lady). The Siparis from Pescasseroli were one of the big sheep-owning families of the Sangro Valley; in addition to the big palaces of Pescasseroli and Alvito, they owned also a palace, lands and manor farms in Foggia.

Hunting was very common and practised against many species of mammals and birds, all listed and described in Luigi Dorotea's book *Della caccia e della pesca nel Caraceno. Sommario Zoologico*; he was a native from Villetta Barrea, a doctor with widespread political, historical, and scientific interests. He was also a hunter and in his book describes the methods of hunting for the different species, including bear and chamois.

Dorotea also talks about wolves, animals "pernicious for their instinct to harm", considered "public enemies by all peoples", thus "persecuted everywhere". As is known, during the first years of the park's foundation, the wolf was considered harmful all over Italy and also in the park, where it was hunted; the pictures of Carlo Paolucci, at that time director of the park, with his *tableaux* of killed wolves, are well-known. Alessandro Ghigi himself wrote that the wolf was a species to eliminate from nature, but added

> As a naturalist, I can wish too that the Italic wolf does not disappear completely, but in order to achieve this, there are two possible ways: reserves in an unpopulated land of the Central or Southern Apennine, allowing the wolves to live undisturbed and killing those that exit to go in the adjoining areas. (Ghigi 1947).

He then suggests that some families of wolves might stay in a big, well-made pit in the zoo of Rome or in Pescasseroli, to maintain the breed.

There were, however, other naturalists who thought in a different way, like Prof. Lino Vaccari, who wrote:

> Even understanding the legitimate concern of the park's administrative board in favouring the development of the species (bear, chamois, and roe deer) to which the park is dedicated; even approving with all my heart the attempt to save the "noble resident game", as a naturalist and a friend of

nature, I cannot and will never be convinced that, to defend some species of animals, it is necessary to exterminate others. (Vaccari 1941).

Wolf protection arrived many years later, with the "St. Francis and the wolf" operation promoted by the WWF, followed by the law that declared the wolf a protected species.

Scientific research before the establishment of the park

Scientific research in the described areas had begun before the establishment of the park due to some naturalists, including the botanist Loreto Grande, whose first publication is dated 1904 and concerns the flora of Villavallelonga, the zoologist Enrico Festa, who in 1914 organised some zoological excursions in the mountains of the Sangro Valley in collaboration with experts of the different groups of animal species, and the geographer Roberto Almagià, with his research in the Comino Valley and on the Marsican mountains.

The Abruzzo chamois was described by Neumann on the basis of a stuffed sample preserved in the Natural History Museum of Genoa which aroused great interest among faunists and hunters. It also interested exponents of the Abruzzo cultural circle such as Leonardo Dorotea and Nestore Tarolla with two faunal contributions, while Uberto D'Andrea published the photograph of a shot chamois on the cover of his book on the history of Villetta Barrea; the year in which the picture was taken is unknown and the caption says: "Chamois hunting in upper Sangro".

The Marsican bear was described in 1921 by Giuseppe Altobello, doctor and zoologist from Campobasso. The bear too was at the centre of local interest, as shown by the many studies and articles on it from the historical and wildlife point of view. It has to be remembered that Erminio Sipari always gave great attention to the fauna of the park in his works (Sipari 1926) and Orano published a photograph of Sipari between a chamois and a bear with this caption: "Erminio Sipari between his protected".

At an international level, the Abruzzo chamois was well-known in the scientific ambit, as witnessed by the French zoologist Marcel Couturier's monograph, published a few years after the foundation of the park, in which the systematic and biogeographic significance of the subspecies *ornata* was emphasised. About the bear, it is enough to remember Couturier's other monograph on the brown bear that talks amply about the Abruzzo National Park and its importance for the protection of the "Altobello bear".

At the International Hunting Exhibition in Berlin in 1937 a Marsican bear and an Abruzzo chamois were exhibited; the bear had been shot in 1910 in Civitella Alfedena and today is in the Zoological Museum of Rome; it is a female specimen and on the sign is written "Gift from H.M. the King", who was Vittorio Emanuele III. In the catalogue is reported the place where the chamois was preserved, the Milizia forestale command of Pescasseroli, but not the year or the place of its killing.

The foundation of the park

The origin of the Abruzzo National Park (now Abruzzo, Lazio and Molise National Park) is directly linked to the pre-existing royal hunting reserve.

In 1860-1861 Leonardo Dorotea from Villetta Barrea launched the idea of a royal hunting reserve to offer to the king Vittorio Emanuele II. This aim was reached in 1872 thanks to the brothers Francesco Saverio and Carmelo Sipari, Erminio's uncle and father respectively, who, with a notarial act dated June 21, 1872 transferred to the king Vittorio Emanuele II, who had expressed his desire for a bear hunt, the hunting reserve on three mountains owned by the Siparis. Immediately, the councils of Opi, Pescasseroli, Villavallelonga, Collelongo, Lecce nei Marsi, Gioia nei Marsi and others resolved to reserve to the King, without limitations, the big game.

The problem of the establishment of the Abruzzo National Park was posed in 1913, when the royal reserve of the upper Sangro Valley was no longer used and the need of a park for the protection of the Apennine chamois and the Marsican bear consequently emerged.

It is easy to notice that the land of Marsica, upper Sangro Valley, Comino Valley, and Mainarde actually held all those essential peculiarities to become a park: mountains, forests, fauna, flora, even if the area was full–particularly in the valley bottoms–of scattered villages. On the other hand, looking at the old photographs of the above mentioned places, two very opposing facts emerge: on the one hand, wide and thick, almost intact, forests; on the other hand, very deteriorated areas, without forest or herbaceous vegetation, and, in addition, cultivated areas. Thus, in these almost extreme conditions a fauna of great value and significance survived, made up of bears, wolves, chamois, wildcats, but also lynxes and roe deer. So, it was possible to create a park, it could be done and, in effect, it was done.

The foundation of the park, however, was not so easy as it might seem, as Nicola Vincenzo Cimini's critical analysis made in 2010 shows.

The role of the national scientific community

The national scientific community participated in the initiative for the establishment of the park together with the scientific and conservationist associations mentioned above and many exponents, among whom stand out the botanist Pietro Romualdo Pirotta (Pavia 1853–Rome 1936) and the zoologist Alessandro Ghigi (Bologna 1875–1970). Pirotta was Botany professor at the University of Rome, after teaching at the University of Pavia; he knew the land of the future park very well because he used to spend the summer in Gioia Vecchio. Ghigi was already a prominent zoologist and Zoology professor at the University of Ferrara and then at that of Bologna.

On appointment of the Ministry of Agriculture, in 1911 Ghigi realised a study "on what can be done in the State inalienable forests", the state-owned forests. The report–entitled *Sul ripopolamento delle foreste inalienabili dello Stato*–was published as annex to the bill "Measures for wildlife conservation" introduced to the Chamber of Deputies on February 19, 1911[1]; in the report, Ghigi writes also about the chamois and the bear, species living in the Abruzzo royal reserve. He is also the author of a survey under the auspices of the Emilia-based Società Pro Montibus et Sylvis on the distribution of mammals target of hunting and he writes about the Abruzzo fauna, including the brown bear and the chamois. It was the first time that in Italy these maps of animals distribution were realised and they also aroused great interest at an international level at the Hunting Exhibition in Vienna.

A year later, Lino Vaccari presents to the Unione Zoologica Italiana an organic and complete speech for the protection of Italy's fauna.

In the same period, the Società Botanica Italiana (SBI) was committed on the nature conservation front. Renato Pampanini, secretary of the SBI wrote in 1911 the essay "Per la protezione della flora italiana" (For the conservation of Italian flora) and in 1912 "Per la protezione dei monumenti naturali in Italia" (For the protection of natural monuments in Italy).

During the meeting in Genoa of October 18, 1912 the Società Botanica Italiana launched the constitution of a Committee that "will lead in Italy the movement for nature conservation to find the most appropriate means for the success of its purpose"; more in detail, one of the points stressed was that of achieving the creation of national parks. The committee included Pietro Romualdo Pirotta, Lorenzo Camerano, Alessandro Ghigi, Renato Pampanini, Lino Vaccari, Saverio Monticelli, and Dante Pantanelli.

On April 12, 1913 a meeting of the Società Botanica Italiana was held in Florence, where Prof. Lino Vaccari presented some procedures undertaken and led by Prof. Pirotta to save from possible alterations the vast lands of forests, pastures, and rocks located to the south-east of the Fucino lake, where the last exemplars of Abruzzo chamois and Marsican bear lived. On this occasion a resolution was approved, which hoped that

> The common owners and the government come to an agreement so that those lands might be preserved in the current conditions and also might actually be used for the foundation of a national park (Italian Botanical Society 1913).

A few years later, in 1917, Prof. Pirotta, who was at the same time president of the Lega nazionale per la protezione dei monumenti naturali and the Società Botanica Italiana, wrote a dossier entitled *Il Parco Nazionale dell'Abruzzo* (The Abruzzo National Park) published in Rome by the Federazione italiana delle Associazioni Pro Montibus ed enti affini (Italian League of Associations for Mountains and similar organisations), in which he described the land from Marsica to the Sangro Valley, up to Scanno, Roccaraso, and the Cinque Miglia plateau and proposed the establishment of "the first national park" of Italy. In 1988 an anastatic reproduction of Pirotta's booklet was made, on occasion of the centenary of the Società Botanica Italiana, and, in the same year, on Franco Tassi's initiative, a commemorative stone for Pirotta was posed on the external wall of the Park Museum in Pescasseroli.

In the first part of his proposal, Pirotta stresses some aspects of the environmental destruction that had taken place in the past centuries, including deforestation "even where it was not necessary". He talks also about the destruction of the flora, distinguishing among plants for essential oil and liqueur, medicinal and ornamental plants, and plants for collections, that is to say for the purpose of study by herbariums. Those are the same categories admitted today and reported in the laws for the protection of flora. Pirotta proposes the creation of "national parks or big reserves" for the conservation and protection of whole and wide areas of the national territory, with all their peculiar natural aspects, the landscape, the flora, the fauna, and the earth.

The second part includes the description of the area, including the flora and fauna, intended for the Abruzzo National Park. The land proposed for the future park is quite extended, as shown in the enclosed map. Today we can see that it coincides with the present park and the external area of protection, as well as some marginal areas such as Castel di Sangro.

In the third part, finally, Pirotta outlines the features that the park should have in the above described area: a large "biological reserve" for the conservation of flora, fauna and landscape. Pirotta's idea of the park is that of a natural reserve of a strictly conservative kind, at scientists' and naturalists' disposal, as we will see shortly.

Pirotta's booklet was presented to the Società Botanica Italiana in Florence at the April 12, 1918 meeting, when Italy was still involved in World War I. The president of the Società Botanica Italiana, Pasquale Baccarini, illustrates Pirotta's plan and then concludes, stressing the importance of the proposal and suggests giving it a vote of support. The agenda is thus approved and appeals

> to the Ministry of Agriculture and the Ministry of Public Instruction so that they allow the foundation, by specific law, in the very beautiful region located among the mountains of Abruzzo, Sannio, and Molise, included between the Fucino and the Sangro Valley, between Sulmona and Picinisco, the National Park, that is the natural monument where the elements of the Italian flora and fauna are concentrated, otherwise they will be perpetually threatened by destruction and where all naturalists may find everything that might satisfy their artistic and scientific interests.

The vote clearly shows the influence of Pirotta.

The proposal of the new park was supported by various naturalists, men of culture, and university professors with articles and comments in the press: Adriano Fiori, Botany professor at the University of Florence, Pasquale Baccarini, President of the Società Botanica Italiana (he succeeded Pirotta), Luigi Parpagliolo (deputy general director of the Ministry of Public Education), Roberto Almagià (Geography professor at the University of Rome), Lino Vaccari[2] (director of the Chanousia alpine botanical garden in Val d'Aosta), Flavio Santi, Ercole Sarti, Renato Pampanini (botanist, in that period secretary of the Società Botanica Italiana), Giuseppe Altobello, Oreste Mattirolo (Botany professor at the University of Turin), Gustavo Giovannoni (Architecture professor at the University of Rome, president of the Roman section of the CAI, at that time he had drawn the plans for the refuges of the park), Giovan Battista Miliani (President of the Pro Montibus et Sylvis Society and minister of Agriculture) and others. Among them, as it is well-known, there was the philosopher Benedetto Croce, Erminio Sipari's cousin and native of Pescasseroli.

These articles refer mainly to the scientific (flora, fauna and earth) and aesthetic (natural beauty) aspects, but also to some of an ecological nature; all of them stress, on the one hand, the importance of conservation of one of Italy's most significant strips of land; on the other hand, the aspects linked to visiting the new future park (i.e. tourism).

Finally, the park was established under private initiative. The Member of Parliament Erminio Sipari was the creator and his activity is today well-known thanks to the works of two historians, Luigi Piccioni and Lorenzo Arnone Sipari.

A few years later, Alessandro Ghigi in a general paper on fauna and hunting in Italy on the occasion of the International Hunting Exhibition in Berlin wrote: "Worthy of special mention are the Abruzzo chamois (*Rupicapra ornata* Neumann) and the Abruzzo bear (*Ursus arctos marsicanus* Altobello), which live in the land of the vast and magnificent national park in the heart of the Marsican region" (Ghigi 1937).

Other contributions of those years that stress the importance of the park and its fauna were published in 1938 by Giuseppe Donzelli, in 1940 by Lino Vaccari, and in 1949 by Lamberto Leporati.

It is important to notice that the scientific community was very attentive when the park was founded; the "Rivista di Biologia" (edited by Gustavo Brunelli, Osvaldo Polimanti, and Vincenzo Rivera) in 1923 published the news of the establishment of the park, with a 1:100,000 scale map and this comment: "We believe that our readers of 'Rivista di Biologia' will appreciate our offer of this clear map of the new national park" (Editorial staff 1923). It was to be the first map of the park. The second was published in Erminio Sipari's *Manuale del Parco* of 1925. The Condotta forestale marsicana (Marsican Forest Office) is represented in both.

Scientific research after the foundation of the park

Once the Abruzzo National Park Authority was formally established–under the extraordinary impulse of Erminio Sipari–it immediately began different activities, as we can read in Sipari's famous and well-known *Relazione*, a classic of Italian literature on parks, written in 1926.

About the national scientific community's contribution at this point of existence of the park, it is necessary to mention the 1933 *Guida del Parco*, edited by the CAI of Rome. It contains a short summary of the naturalistic knowledge of the park, with the contributions of Roberto Almagià (Orography and Morphology), Camillo Crema (Geology), Giuseppe Lepri (Fauna), Pietro Romualdo Pirotta (Flora) and others on hiking and skiing.

In the 1930s, when the guide was published, Prof. Pirotta could admire the Abruzzo National Park, organised and working in all the beauty of its forests, flora and fauna. For the guide of the CAI, he writes "when all has been done" and cannot avoid describing again locations and landscapes, mountains and valleys, flora and vegetation, with a renewed and growing admiration, and an enthusiasm almost greater than at the time of the first proposals and battles for the park. Certainly, also on this occasion the main reference is of an aesthetic nature, however at the end of the work of 1933 we can read some clear and enlightening phrases, still true today, with a precise reference to the safeguard of the mountains and their environment "[...] the forests and mountains are not waiting for big hotels or tennis courts, or mount-profaners [...]"

In the few and spare words of Pirotta there is the meaning of the conservationist battle developed some decades later in the Abruzzo National Park and in the other Italian national parks. Since then, an evolution has occurred in the knowledge and definition of the reasons validating the creation of parks; yesterday they were more aesthetic and today they are more ecological and sociological, but in essence very little changes before the idea of the parks and the need to preserve the most important areas of our planet.

In the same period, research activity in the park restarts with the contributions of Adriano Fiori in 1927, Loreto Grande in 1925, and Wilczek and Vaccari in 1940 for botany and of Paolo Luigioni from 1929 onwards for entomology. Luigioni will discover a new species of coleopteran that he named after the creator of the park, the *Chrysochloa sipari.*

Scientific research in the area of the park had a great development in the post-war years, with the establishment, due to Franco Tassi, of the Ecological Apennine Studies Centre with specific work-groups organised according to species and subjects (chamois, bear, wolf, etc.).

The problems of the park (lakes and other issues)

The Abruzzo National Park almost immediately faced big problems with the proposal of construction of two artificial basins for hydroelectric power purposes in the upper Sangro Valley; Erminio Sipari strongly opposed this plan, basing his opinion of that of the geologist Michele Gortani. Finally, only the basin of Barrea was built and the plain of Opi, of great landscape and botanic relevance, was saved.

A few years after the establishment of the Park, Prof. Pirotta was involved in a situation that led him to resign from the Park administrative board, after a logging request in Val Fondillo. His resignation was rejected, but never recalled by Pirotta, who was replaced by Loreto Grande.

Altobello (1922) felt he had to intervene on the logging issue:

In the meantime, while the park is gradually slowly establishing itself, the axe of the woodcutter over and over again and relentlessly everywhere in those forests hits and destroys the most beautiful specimens of our woody vegetation, beats furiously on those ancient logs, razing the most beautiful ornament offered to us by the earth, destroying a whole world of living beings, plants and animals, which has its life in the forest.

Nicola Cimini as well was very critical, but objective, with the logging issue in his 2010 volume on the *Lands of the Bear*.

At that time it was impossible to talk about a park "policy" for forests (even if we have to remember that Erminio Sipari founded the Condotta forestale marsicana), but in the post-war years the Abruzzo National Park was the first Italian park to lease from the municipalities areas to protect from logging. These actions were adopted afterwards by the Stelvio and Gran Paradiso parks, while the new parks, until now, have not shown a great sensitivity on this issue, which is essential both for its conservationist aspect and the relationship between park and municipalities. This is proved by the Engadine Swiss National Park, whose land is entirely leased by the park and where conflicts between the park and the inhabitants have never been reported.

The end of the first period of existence of the park

After so much enthusiasm and effort, the first period of life of the Abruzzo National Park ended negatively on 1935, when Erminio Sipari was ousted as president and the Milizia forestale took over the park. After the war, Sipari was never again involved in the park matter by Italy's new political class. He was the first of many presidents and directors of parks ousted from their office because they were really committed to park preservation and thus not appreciated; these were Erminio Sipari, Francesco Saltarelli, and Franco Tassi in Abruzzo; Ugo Bayer and Renzo Videsott at the Gran Paradiso; and Walter Frigo at the Stelvio. A cruel and hasty method, but effective and practical!

The national scientific community and the park

The national scientific community participated in the promotion and foundation of the Abruzzo National Park with two different approaches, in two different ways, and precisely with scientific research, supplying data and information for the scientific knowledge of park land and with a strictly conservationist contribution through the support votes of scientific associations and the comments of a personal nature. The group of pioneers included remarkable idealists like Pampanini, Vaccari, Pirotta, and Ghigi, even if he was also very pragmatic.

This double position of Italian science asserted itself in the post-war period, when Renzo Videsott in 1946 obtained from the Consiglio Nazionale delle Ricerche (National Research Council, CNR) the establishment of a Committee for national parks, transformed a few years later by Alessandro Ghigi in to the Commission for nature and its resource conservation of the Consiglio Nazionale delle Ricerche. Members of the commission were Renzo Videsott, Roberto Corti, Sergio Tonzig, Valerio Giacomini and others. Its commitment to save some threatened places in Italy is well-known, Val di Genova and Tovel Lake for example, and more recently Porto Tolle. These interventions certainly created some bother, so, after Ghigi's death, the Commission was abolished by the CNR.

With this act, still impossible to understand and therefore to accept, the CNR (and with it the whole national scientific community) entrenched itself at an exclusively technical-scientific level. In the following years there were evaluations, surveys, and so on, but all of them limited to a technical level; even scientific associations contributed to the realisation of surveys more than legitimate and necessary, but without that idealistic impulse that distinguished the pioneer years. The actions of a conservationist and preservationist nature were delegated only to the new environmentalist associations which have appeared in the meanwhile in our country and to a few isolated people.

Conclusion

The Congress on the ninety years of the Abruzzo National Park falls in an especially hard time for our country, a period of serious political decay and also, I would add, of cultural decay in the ambit of national parks, even if with some exceptions. The distance from the main aims of the parks and the original idea of the park has increased and public opinion is really confused about what parks are, how they should work and what they should effectively be. And the responsibility of what has happened in part falls on some members of the environmentalist world.

The 2012 Pescasseroli Conference, dedicated to the first Italian national park, although at the beginning established under private initiative might be the occasion to re-launch the idea of parks for a greater achievement and an effective presence in our country.

Bibliography

Altobello, Giuseppe. 2006 (manuscript 1922). La Regione del Parco Nazionale d'Abruzzo. In Mauro Ferri, Corrado Guacci, Guido Venturi, Claudio Bertarelli, L'Altobello ritrovato, *Atti della Società dei Naturalisti e Matematici di Modena* 87: 77-104.

Cimini, Nicola Vincenzo. 2010. *Genesi, vita e storia delle Terre dell'Orso. Con uno sguardo alla Terra di Opi.* Opi: Nicola Vincenzo Cimini.

Ghigi, Alessandro. 1937. Italia. In *Amtlicher Führer und Katalog der Internationalen Jagdausstellung Berlin 1937 2. bis 28. November*, 49-52. Berlin: Reichsbund Deutsche Jägerschaft–Neudamm.

—. 1947. *Fauna e caccia*. Bologna: Edagricole.

Pirotta, Romualdo. 1917. *Il Parco Nazionale dell'Abruzzo.* Rome: Federazione italiana delle Associazioni Pro Montibus ed enti affini.

—. 1933. La flora. In *Il Parco Nazionale d'Abruzzo*, 79-83. Rome: Club Alpino Italiano–Section of Rome.

Redazione. 1923. Il Parco Nazionale degli Abruzzi. *Rivista di Biologia* s. V, n. 1: 138.

Sipari, Erminio. 1926. Caratteristiche della fauna della regione del parco. In Erminio Sipari, *Relazione del Presidente del direttorio provvisorio dell'Ente Autonomo del Parco Nazionale d'Abruzzo alla Commissione Amministratrice dell'ente stesso, nominata con Regio Decreto 25 marzo 1923*, 17-52. Tivoli: Maiella.

Società Botanica Italiana. 1913. Ordine del giorno per la costituzione di un Parco Nazionale in Abruzzo. *Bullettino della Società Botanica Italiana* 4: 59-60.

Vaccari, Lino. 1921. Necessità di un parco nazionale in Italia. *Le Vie d'Italia* 5: 489-495.

—. 1941. Considerazioni intorno al Parco Nazionale d'Abruzzo. *Rivista di Biologia* 31: 266-284.

Notes

1. In the same years, the botanist Renato Pampanini was also interested in the state forests and proposed to use them for the establishment of natural reserves.

2. Lino Vaccari's article "Necessità di un parco nazionale in Italia" was published in the review "Le Vie d'Italia" of the Touring Club Italiano. The Touring, however, thought it opportune to put at the beginning of Vaccari's article a note saying frankly that "this plan [of a national park in Abruzzo] neither practically resolves the problem, nor, if accepted, achieves the ideal aims. In the imminence of the plan's discussion it could be interesting to objectively expose the serious

doubts that it inspires". This was written due to the president of the Touring, Luigi Vittorio Bertarelli, thus opening a harsh debate which was resolved in favour of the conservationists of the time.

THE NATIONAL PARK
AND THE AMERICAN EXPERIENCE

JAMES SIEVERT

Arriving in Abruzzo National Park reminds me of being on the road to Yosemite, the slow climb from the heat and dust of the flatlands of California's Central Valley until you pass through various types of forest, first the oaks and then the pines, to arrive in green Yosemite Valley. It is a similar rise from the flatlands of Fucino outside Abruzzo National Park until you arrive in the green meadows of the Val di Sangro.

I am not the only American who has felt the pull of Abruzzo National Park over the years, however. In the 1920s several U.S. National Park officials made the trip to the verdant fields of the Val di Sangro to see exactly what type of national park the Italians had founded.

Ansel Hall, a naturalist for the Park Service, said that Italy "seems by far to be more advanced than any other European nation in its enthusiasm for national parks" after visiting Abruzzo National Park in 1924.

The botanist Harvey M. Hall (unrelated to Ansel Hall) embarked on a European tour in 1928, visiting national parks in Switzerland, Poland and Sweden, as well as Abruzzo National Park. He came at a time when Americans were wondering what the purpose of their own parks was. His report noted the strong focus on science in most European national parks. He mentioned Italy as a place where tourist organizations had a big influence on the creation of parks.

Which brings us to the story of the first national park. Yellowstone is the icon. In September 1870 a group of men sat around a campfire in Yellowstone. They were inspired by the natural beauty around them, so they decided not to exploit the landscape for profit. Instead, they urged the U.S. federal government to protect the landscape as a public park. Altruism was the basis for national parks–giving up private gain for the collective good.

It is a nice story. But it is not true. Like all first causes, the origin of the national park idea remains vague. A more likely creation story, and one closer to the truth, is this: the expanding railroad companies of the United

States created Yellowstone. For tourism. For a profit motive. Tourism was an attractive business investment. It was economic development.

Whatever the origin of the national park idea, its influence spread rapidly around the world, including Italy. For example, the industrialist Giambattista Miliani published an article in 1907, following his trip to the United States, in which he wrote that national parks could and should be imitated in Italy and elsewhere. The purpose, he wrote, was to save natural beauty from destruction.

Exactly fifty years after the founding of Yellowstone, Abruzzo National Park was created in 1922. Abruzzo was founded with the American model in mind–a place that included both recreation and the protection of natural beauty.

Abruzzo was not a wilderness, of course, in the American sense. The human presence was felt very strongly in the territory of the park, as it was everywhere in Italy. But the presence of two big fauna–the brown bear and the chamois–gave the Abruzzo Park a certain cachet that other parks could not boast. Abruzzo National Park was also similar to the early American parks in another way: the early park leadership under Erminio Sipari did not shy away from promoting both the cultural and natural aspects of the Abruzzo Park.

The first three decades of the twentieth century were a vital period in the establishment of Europe's early national parks. Some of these protected areas, such as the Swiss National Park, were established on the basis of ecology. The Swiss park was not for recreation, but for scientific research.

In Italy, too, some of the strongest backers of national parks came from the scientific community. The biologist Lino Vaccari, for example, championed the creation of wilderness zones where nature could develop unmolested. Vaccari was a tireless advocate for nature protection in Italy. But his vision of wilderness zones was impractical. In fact, his vision was not even in line with the mission of Yellowstone. He saw national parks as scientific reserves; the first U.S. parks were for protecting natural beauty. Not surprisingly, the creation of the Swiss park had a big impact on Vaccari.

The mission of Yellowstone and the other early American national parks was to open up these areas of natural beauty to the people. The development of parks for tourism and the management of nature in the parks did not run contrary to the American economic system. The national parks were a cooperative effort between government and private business to create an economic base for tourism. Tourism was more important than nature protection.

When the National Park Service began in 1916, it was not a scientific bureau. It emphasized access, roads, campgrounds, infrastructure. Its leaders saw the national parks as pleasure grounds. Natural resource management was second to tourism. The national parks were preserved for scenery–in Italian *bellezze naturali*–not for wildlife management. In fact, the idea of wildlife management did not exist until the 1920s and 1930s.

There is more than just a little irony in the fact that ecological attitudes achieved prominence in the early European national parks, while in the American parks the priority was on tourism and natural beauty. An interesting question that merits further investigation is whether the travel to Europe by American naturalists and National Park officials in the 1920s had any impact on the National Park Service's turn towards a more scientific outlook.

Of course, for the natural world to remain beautiful, it required some measure of protection. In this intersection between nature protection and infrastructure development, Abruzzo National Park was more like American national parks than it was like many of the European parks. The big difference between Abruzzo and U.S. parks, of course, was that people lived productive lives in the area of the Abruzzo park. People were also living in some U.S. national parks, such as Yosemite in California. But these inhabitants–native Americans–were removed when the parks were established.

The option of removal was not available in Italy, of course. And yet, apart from this issue, the path that Erminio Sipari and the early leaders of Abruzzo chose was similar to the early U.S. parks. Sipari searched for a balance between tourism and nature protection. He called this balance *civiltà nelle montagne*–a beautiful phrase that succinctly sums up the situation. Sipari's own mission statement was one of the most precise formulations written anywhere at that time about the role of a national park.

"The two purposes of a national park–the conservation of wildlife and the development of tourism–are not incompatible in the least," Sipari wrote.

What did Sipari mean by *civiltà nelle montagne?* He meant opening up the Abruzzo mountains to the outside world, not to destroy the mountains, but to save them. The more culture that came to the mountains–and by culture he also meant highways, hotels, electric power and modern civilization–the more people would come to enjoy the natural and cultural life of Abruzzo. The more people saw this natural beauty, the more they would be inspired to save it from radical alteration. Or at least develop it in a way that was not too destructive for the natural world.

National parks may have been America's best idea for the rest of the world. But in the early twentieth century, Harvey M. Hall wrote:

> Our warning as to danger of delay comes from the experience in Europe. The problem there is much more difficult than with us, for they no longer have extensive natural areas to protect. They must first recreate natural conditions through long periods of protection, sometimes accompanied by replanting and by reintroduction of the indigenous fauna. There, leaders speak of a "grandiose experiment to create a wilderness", whereas we need only to protect the wilderness that we already possess. Our task is to preserve what such people as the Swiss and the Italians strive to re-create.

In the case of Abruzzo National Park, however, it was not a question of recreating wilderness. As Erminio Sipari clearly saw, it was a question of emphasizing a new spirit that saw the economic and environmental value of the culture of the mountain environment.

Though the initial years of Abruzzo National Park saw the continued slaughter of wolves under Sipari, the brown bears that inhabited the Apennine mountains in and around the park were finally spared the assault of hunters. (Wolves did not gain any protection until the late 1960s with the new management of the national park under Franco Tassi). Sipari believed, as did his cousin Benedetto Croce, the famous Italian philosopher who was born in Pescasseroli in the park, that the bears, too, belonged to the culture of the mountains.

The continued existence of the bears in the national park, their tenacious will to survive, is a testimony to harmonious relations that can develop in protected areas over the years between humans and the natural world. In a nod to Edward O. Wilson's biophilia hypothesis, we could even speculate that the bears have developed a certain instinctive affection for humans in Abruzzo National Park. They know where they are loved and protected. And in turn, the bears might love us more than we will ever know.

Bibliography

Hall, Harvey M.1929. European Reservations for the Protection of Natural Conditions. *Journal of Forestry* 6: 667-684.

Keller, Robert H. and Michael F. Turek. 1999. *American Indians and National Parks*. Tucson: University of Arizona Press.

Miliani, Giovanni Battista. 1907. Il grande parco nazionale di Yellowstone. *Nuova Antologia* 1.5.1907: 98-112.

Sellars, Richard West. 1997. *Preserving Nature in the National Parks. A History*. New Haven (Ct): Yale University Press.

Sipari, Erminio. 1926. *Relazione del Presidente del Direttorio provvisorio dell'Ente autonomo del Parco nazionale d'Abruzzo alla Commissione amministratrice dell'Ente stesso, nominata con Regio Decreto 25 marzo 1923*. Tivoli: Maiella.

Vaccari, Lino .1921. Il Parco Nazionale del Gran Paradiso. *Le vie d'Italia* 12: 1255-1263.

Faunal Knowledge and Policies at the Origins of the Park and in Its First Period

Corradino Guacci

Before approaching this topic, I would like to address a grateful thought to two people whose death still causes a sense of bewilderment that I feel when I come back to Pescasseroli and walk in the town's main square. The first is Francesco Coccia who, with the historical memory, both his own and that inherited from his father Leucio, head guard from the 1930s to the 1960s, gave me precious explanations and rewarded me with his friendship. The second is uncle Armando Petrella, I say uncle not for kinship but as an appellation used in our land, a way to express at the same time both affection and respect. Many things could and should be said about him, but, for obvious reasons, all I will remember is his light hearted, disarming, and sometimes slightly ironic smile, with which he welcomed us warmly when we came back to the Park. Thanks, thus, to them, but also to the inhabitants of the valleys and to the head guards who, in the last ninety years, have worked in silence and in the background, allowing us to enjoy, still today, this extraordinary heritage that is our Abruzzo Park.

To the question "Why was the Abruzzo Park established right in this valley and not in another place", I think the answer has to be sought mainly in the peculiarity of the land and in its centuries-old isolation. The mountainous Abruzzo has often been represented, especially in the past, stressing the roughness of climate and landscape. The rough orography of its mountains always influenced the image proposed by geographers, until it became a stereotype similar to that which praises the temperament, interpreted as physical and moral strength, of the people who inhabited them.

Leandro Alberti, geographer and traveller from Bologna, in his *Descrittione di tutta Italia* published in the mid-sixteenth century, proposes two attractive etymological interpretations linked to the nature of the region. The first is that Abruzzo originates from *Asprutio*, due to, as

Alberti says, the "great ruggedness of the mountains there", (maybe from Latin *abruptum* = steep place, cliff, or from *asper* = wild, inaccessible). The second, from *Aprutium* as derivation from *aper* = boar, because, still citing the geographer, "this village seems almost the home of boars for the shady forest and the thick woods, which here are very abundant" ("parendo questo paese quasi una habitatione da Cinghiali per le ombrose selve e fitti boschi, che quivi sono in grand'abondanza"). This cliché is often well-represented in the old scrolls. This rough morphology allowed the Abruzzo-Molise Apennine to have an effective role of defence of the northern borders of the Kingdom of Naples. It protected the borders, as well as giving refuge to surviving examples of the great Apennine mammal fauna that sheltered here, threatened by the advance of humans.

We have to consider that, between the end of the eighteenth and the beginning of the nineteenth century, due to the 1764 and 1817 famines and the subversion of feudality in 1806, there was a remarkable acceleration of the logging process in order to have new cultivable lands, made even more incisive by the adaptability to high altitudes of the new species of agronomic interest from the American continent, such as potatoes, corn and beans able to colonise the mountain slopes up to 1500-1600 meters of altitude. Sipari, in his *Relazione*, a fundamental document for understanding the origin of the Abruzzo Park, mentions the *cacchiti* understood as tangled forests, the *appicchi* which are the vertical rocky faces, the *scatafosce* impenetrable canyons and deep valleys, the *cantonere* single or clustered erratic boulders reminders of old glaciations, stressing the fundamental role played in the survival of bear and chamois (Sipari 1926, p. 218).

The lack of a relevant road system, then, favoured the conditions for the plateaux isolations, whose crossing, until the second half of the nineteenth century, was possible thanks to the thousand-year-old shepherd tracks like the Pescasseroli-Candela, the Castel di Sangro-Lucera, or the Celano-Foggia, whose route was largely adopted from the famous Via degli Abruzzi that from L'Aquila, along the Aterno valley, arrived at Sulmona and from there clambered up to the Cinquemiglia plateau and then descended to Roccaraso, toward Castel di Sangro, Isernia, Venafro in the direction of Naples along the Volturno. This land was so wild that those who were obliged to travel through the Cinquemiglia in the eighteenth century, especially in winter, used to dictate their last will and testament beforehand. For those coming from Naples, the capital of the Kingdom, "civilization" ended in Castel di Sangro, so that news of bear hunting, in the ancien régime, came from this area where the Neapolitan court found adequate hospitality for its needs. The frequentations of

Alfonso II of Aragon, duke of Calabria, go back to that time, when, in 1476, under the rule of his father Ferrante I, he stayed in Castel di Sangro for "the fresh air and the bear hunting" ("lo ayro frisco e la caccia de li urci").

However, the forays of princes and rulers were an exception because, due to the distance from Naples and the poor road connections, the bear was a prerogative mainly of the local lords. The hunting parties on the Morrone of Restaino Cantelmo, count of Popoli, "who was so strong, arduous, and valorous, that until his old age sought bears in the hunt and killed them" ("che fu di tante forze, di tanto ardire e di tanto valore, che fin alla vecchiezza andava a incontrar gli orsi a caccia e gli uccideva") in the fifteenth and sixteenth centuries are remembered, together with those which have the Sagittario Valley as backdrop and Antonio Belprato, lord of Anversa, and Don Titta di Capua, lord of Scanno and later of Anversa as leading characters (Sipari 1926, p. 20). Hereafter, bear hunting, freed of feudal restrictions, was practised by a few bold and solitary bear hunters or by hunting groups of local notables, the only ones who could afford the costs of such organisation. We have to think that, between the nineteenth and the twentieth centuries, the hunting arranged in honour of the princes of the House of Savoy, required 60 to 80 beaters. Only towards the end of the eighteenth century a road network took shape, able to break, finally, the isolation of the upper Val di Sangro: the completion of the connection between Pescina and the Marsica of the Fucino area in the 1880s, that with Alfedena and between the upper Volturno and the Val di Sangro in 1883, and the opening to the Ciociaria through the Forca d'Acero pass in 1894.

So the mountain, thanks to its marginality, was often the last refuge for animal species threatened by hunting activities, as happened to the symbol of alpine fauna, the ibex, considered extinct at the beginning of the nineteenth century due to ruthless hunting. When, in 1821, a small residual population, protected in the deep valleys on the slopes of the Gran Paradiso was found, king Charles Felix issued some royal licenses to forbid its hunting in all lands of the Kingdom of Sardinia. Obviously, the royal decree's priority was not the protection of an endangered animal, but the guarantee for the King to have exclusive hunting. Nevertheless, in many cases it was the hunting egoism of the powerful that assured the safety of important species of Italian fauna, as shown, for example, by the system of protected areas in Piedmont and Val d'Aosta, born from Vittorio Emanuele II's passion for the hunt.

And now, I think the time has come for a reflection that leads to revising the interpretation, completely negative, of exclusive rights, rather reconsidering the involuntary role of protection, ahead of its time, represented by these reserves. Let us think of what happened here in the upper Sangro when, after the transfer of the hunting rights on their mountains to the hunter King by the brothers Sipari, Carmelo and Francesco Saverio, many communities of the valley followed their example, giving birth to the Savoy hunting reserves in the Central Apennine. So, in April of 1873, the first reserve was born, even if it had a short life and was abolished in March 1878 after Vittorio Emanuele II's death and the indifference to hunting of his successor, Umberto I.

This reserve was followed by another dedicated to Vittorio Emanuele III, who came here to hunt in 1899 when he was already Prince of Naples. It was inaugurated in 1900, but met with the antipathy of the King's Great Hunter, Giulio Carminati di Brambilla, who defined it "a joke of a reserve". Then, the continuous complaints of the sheep-owners for the damage caused by bears and their relative considerable claims for compensation led, at the end of 1912, to its abolition. On this matter, the zoologist Giuseppe Altobello, about whom we will talk again, stressed, with a certain sarcasm, that the bear had suddenly changed its eating habits becoming a "dangerous carnivorous animal just when the reserve was established: then all the cows in danger, all the goats and calves, all the sheep devoured by wolves became the many victims of the bears for the reimbursement of the damage from the Royal House administration, which in the last year paid up to £70,000 of indemnities!" (Altobello 1921, p. 17)

Now, apart from their short life, it is indubitable that this suspension of the indiscriminate hunting activity, together with the pause after World War I, were providential for the great Apennine fauna preservation also because, between the end of the nineteenth and the beginning of the twentieth centuries, firearms begin to spread amongst all social classes, no longer a prerogative of a hunting élite, and their technology underwent a great acceleration. We find this role confirmed in the outcome of the survey reported in the end notes of the *Relazione* that, even if incomplete, presents significant elements. During the five years of the first reserve the killing of five bears was recorded; during the five years soon after the abolition, fourteen bears were shot in the upper Sangro alone, as many were killed by the hunter Antonio Orazi from Gioia de' Marsi, watchman of the herds of cav. Alessi, an important sheep-owner of the zone. Much more evident was the impact of the abolition which occurred in 1912. Also in this case only five shot bears were recorded in twelve years; in the following ten years, from 1913 to 1923, when the Park was officially founded, the bears killed by hunters were forty-four, ten in 1921 alone, of which six in Pescasseroli. In the same period the chamois too suffered for the re-opening of hunting: on one day of January 1913, fifteen specimens were shot, of a total of forty-nine recorded in eighty-five years of statistics.

The echo provoked by this massacre, together with the small number of survivors limited to the areas around Civitella Alfedena and Opi, and, not least, the assignment of the status of endemic species of Abruzzo, with the name of *Rupicapra ornata*, probably were the reasons that facilitate the prompt issue of the hunting ban, put in effect by the January 9, 1913 Royal Decree. The bear, on the other hand, would have to wait until 1939, when the act on hunting–the so-called Acerbo Act–would ban it, stopping, among other things, that practice, described with masterly skill by Piccioni in his "Il dono dell'orso", that saw it as a precious resource of the Valley offered as a token to the powerful person of the moment (Piccioni 1996). Evidence of this are the hunting rights donated to the Savoys, the skins sent to kings and notables, and the big game hunt. Among these are one in 1899 in honour of the Prince of Naples and future King Vittorio Emanuele III; one in 1907 in Villavallelonga, dedicated to him as well; one in 1921 organised for H.R.H. Amedeo of Aosta Duke of Apulia; finally, those of 1931 and 1933 offered to the high hierarchy of the National Fascist Party and the Milizia forestale nazionale (National Forestry Militia).

Moreover, the bear lacked that exclusivity later conferred after by the studies of Giuseppe Altobello, doctor and naturalist from Molise (Guacci 1995), who, on the basis of some morphological and especially craniometrical observations, gave it in 1921 the status of endemic subspecies of the Central-Southern Apennine, naming it *Ursus arctos marsicanus*. This peculiarity, among other things, completely escaped the notice of renowned zoologists such as Alessandro Ghigi, Enrico Festa or Giuseppe Lepri, appointed in 1923 as zoologist in the administrative board of the Park Authority. This role would have been more suitable to Altobello's competence, as a great expert of the fauna of that region, of which he gathered a wide collection of specimens: 2,240 birds, 510 mammals, 270 reptiles, 80 amphibians, 120 fishes, and 540 craniums, essential for comparative studies. A collection defined by Ghigi as "the richest local collection that I have ever seen". However, Lepri, marquise of Rota, belonging to the Roman aristocracy, surely had important liaisons both in the Vatican, as he was a member of the Pontifical Academy of Science in the Vatican and not of the lay Accademia dei Lincei, as well as in the circles of the Savoy court.

Furthermore, at the time of the *Relazione*, knowledge of the bear was very confused, Sipari still talks about two species of bears living in the Park, the *cavallina*, mainly vegetarian, and the *porcina* which prefers meat. To explain the double presence, Sipari remembers that he initially traced the episode cited by Pietro Colletta in his *Storia del Reame di Napoli* about the bears given by the Tsar of Russia, in 1821, to Ferdinand I king of the two Sicilies, who brought them to Italy "to improve the species of bears that lives, little prolific and miserable, in the forest of Abruzzo", but then discovered unsatisfactory due to the lack of confirmation in the archive of the Bourbon reserves, and makes his the theory of the hydrographical basins expressed by the German zoologist Matschie (Sipari 1926, pp. 22-27).

The Bourbons, among other things, did not possess hunting reserves in the upper Sangro, the nearest were the royal hunting grounds of Venafro (Torcino and Mastrati in the countryside around Capriati al Volturno), and that of Montedimezzo between Vastogirardi and San Pietro Avellana in the upper Molise, on the borderline with the Castel di Sangro land. Even if there were contacts with the areas of the Valley: in effect, when Ferdinand IV stayed in Venafro for the hunting in Torcino, the masters of hound were sent to Villetta Barrea to find trout and partridges for the King's table. The late local historian Uberto D'Andrea had noticed, examining the council books of accounts of Villetta Barrea, some payments in favour of two messengers who, on November 7 and December 1, 1791, had brought orders about "the ban of shooting of the bears" in view of an expected hunt of the King (D'Andrea 1981, pp. 104-105). Or like the announcement issued by the Prince of Tarsia on request of the Duke of Miranda to ban hunting and wood collecting in the forests of Cinquemiglia, Pietransieri, Lami, Camarda, and in the Tenimento di S. Pietro Avellana to allow the King to hunt bears in those places (Mascilli Migliorini 1994).

The wolf too, the other protagonist of the faunal events of those years, was honoured by the zoologist Altobello with the status of endemic subspecies with the name of *Canis lupus italicus*. However, this recognition did not save it, unlike the bear and the chamois, from ruthless persecution. At that time, in effect, the decline of transhumance and the consequent transformation of the ovine holding from herd industry to subsistence economy made the damage caused by wolves less and less acceptable and sustainable. As a consequence, in a general impoverishment framework of the Abruzzo mountains, it was easy to identify in the predator a convenient scapegoat. Besides the traditional plunder of herds, the wolf was considered responsible also for the decreasing growth of the populations of chamois, roe deer, and even bears, affirming that the wolves in winter killed all young bears born at the beginning of the year.

Sipari, who knew well the moods of that pastoral society, immediately took the opportunity to gain consensus for the Park policy by indicating the predator. Thus, the wolf became the target of a cruel extermination campaign, promoted with the payment of prizes, so that the first action of the provisional Directorate was the creation, in March 1922, of a prize of 150 lire for every adult specimen shot. In May 1923 the administrative board, as soon as it was installed, issued the first announcement for the destruction of vermin that introduced another prize of 50 lire for the capture of a young wolf or an eagle and 25 lire for a fox.

But an "effective" action to destroy wolves was hindered by the law on hunting, that did not allow their capture after the end of the hunting season, from January 1 to August 15, just the period when, as Sipari stressed, "due to the presence of snow on the high peaks, hungry wolves and foxes come down near the villages and so can be more easily killed with the help of traps and poisoned food". Thanks to the good services of which Sipari, member of Parliament since 1913, benefited in the palaces of Rome, on December 15, 1923 the minister Orso Mario Corbino signed the decree that authorised the hunting of vermin, by any means, also in time of ban. In February 1924, a second announcement, that maintained unchanged the prizes, extended the group of vermin, to include the wildcat, the otter, all the Mustelidae (martens, polecats, and weasels), the eagle owl, falcons and Corvidae in general. A year later, with the commitment of the Ministry of National Economy to refund the costs of the campaign for the destruction of vermin, Sipari increased the number of the municipalities where the prizes were paid, from 18 to 70, and introduced a special prize of 250 lire for the killing of female wolves. Now, if we consider that at that time the Natural History museums of Milan, Turin, Genoa, and Rome paid, for every fat and well-preserved wolf 200-300 lire, the proceeds from the killing of a wolf could reach nearly 500 lire. An important sum, if we think that, at that time, the monthly wage of the director of the Park was 1,500 lire.

Sipari, among other things, to make easier the fight against the vermin, was in contact with the Associazione nazionale Bandite e Riserve d'Italia (National Association of Sanctuaries and Reserves of Italy) that, with the sending of a certain number of gamekeepers expert in the use of traps and poison, would have made a wolf-clearing operation and trained the local population. This hypothesis of collaboration vanished, in December 1923, due to the approaching appointment of the Park director, office filled by the naturalist from Ancona Carlo Paolucci, whose degree in Natural Science and whose long-time hunting curriculum made appealing to external professionals unnecessary. However, after the first encouraging results, the hunting of vermin seemed to come to a sudden stop despite Sipari's activism, which entailed, buying traps in France from specialised companies and getting the best strychnine available on the market, especially the sulphate considered more effective than the nitrate used at the beginning but which did not give satisfactory results.

It was then that the idea of calling experts in the use of poison and traps regained strength, also to overcome the resistance of the director Paolucci, who feared possible accidents from selling strychnine and lending traps to the local population. So, in September 1924, Paolucci contacted the Hunt Office of the French Ministry of Agriculture which addressed him to the Association of lieutenants of the *Louveterie*, an institution already established at the time of Charlemagne and specialised in wolf hunting. The news of the arrival of the French, published in the hunting magazines aroused a certain discontent among the Abruzzo hunters, who affirmed that the Park should have facilitated and organised game hunting for the local wolf hunters, instead of asking abroad. Finally, two French experts came to Abruzzo: a lieutenant of the *Louveterie*, Mr Antoine Merigonde, and his assistant, Baptiste Laborderie, both from Souillac in the Midi-Pyrénées. They worked between January and February 1925, assisted by Paolucci, Tarolla and some consuls of the Park, but with unsatisfying results, apart from two mules poisoned in the area of Lecce de Marsi which cost 2,000 lire of transaction to the Park. The two *louvetiers*, maybe driven by a sense of guilt, said that they were available to come to Abruzzo the following year at their own expense.

After this disappointing experience, the old idea of involving local hunters, providing them with all means to fight the vermin, prevailed. Furthermore, the new course was favoured by the leaving, in January 1926, of the difficult Paolucci and the appointment as director of the more tractable Nicola Tarolla, another man from the Valley, and thus with a local vision certainly more suitable to the strategies carried out by Sipari. This joined commitment of foresters and wolf hunters led to the capture, between 1923 and 1933, of 209 wolves: 84 male, 82 female, and 43 cubs.

If considered from a conservationist viewpoint, the faunal policy of the Park of those years was undoubtedly puzzling. The pillars on which it was grounded were essentially two: the substitution of natural selection with the human one and the unrelenting struggle against the wolf. A line of action designed and supported by Sipari, who said that it was not "the case to be byzantine either on the distinction of useful animals and vermin, or natural equilibrium or harmony among different organisms, for which even predatory animals have their role and their reason for being", (Sipari 1926, p. 224).

A policy that appeared in all its clarity more in the administration of the bear than in that of the wolf, if we think that the same constitutive law of the Park allowed the shooting of bears during the hunts organised by the

Park Authority in order to have an income in its registers. Or like the announced program on the capture of young bears that, inspired by the same economic purpose, was justified by the certainty that in winter the cubs would be eaten by wolves; thus it was more convenient to gain a profit, in that European zoological gardens wanted cubs of Marsican bears.

In all this it has to be remembered that the scientific circle of the time acted peremptorily to save bears and chamois, but this mobilization, which Sipari formally joined, was opportunely used to achieve the aim pursued for a long time: the establishment of the Abruzzo Park and the subsequent economic development of the Valley that, in Sipari's intention, was related more to tourism development than to the protection of flora and fauna, as he admitted in more than one correspondence (Arnone Sipari 1998, p. 62). A vision that Sipari pointed out in 1924, when he prefigured the Abruzzo Park as "an endless public garden […] that should become over the years a big sports field […] and might become a mountain holiday resort for the great clientele from Rome, Naples, and Apulia", (Sipari 1924). This project was not the result of unawareness, because the basis for a correct and modern management of a protected area was well-known: there were the examples of the Swiss National Park of Engadine, founded in August 1914 and Gran Paradiso, and the solicitations coming from the scientific community were also pressing, like the concerned and clearly premonitory appeal of the biologist Lino Vaccari, (Vaccari 1912).

But this knowledge was bent to the need of Sipari's project, to that strategy of economic development of the Valley, that allowed not only hunting but also the use of the forests: an anthropocentric view that was, among other things, the cause of harsh disagreement and resounding breaches: the first was with the botanist Pietro Romualdo Pirotta on the famous logging in Val Fondillo, considered by him too damaging and which led him to resign from the administrative board; then, that with Carlo Paolucci on the capture of young bears and, more in general, on the "naturalistic" management of the Park, and finally, the exclusion of Giuseppe Altobello, too expert and with too strong a personality to be easily influenced.

Without doubt, if it is read in this way, the period of the foundation of the Park could lead to a critical interpretation of Sipari's intervention, but this would be ungenerous because, even if it was reprehensible from the conservationist viewpoint, actions have to be framed in what was a dream, perhaps visionary, but extremely modern: to allow Pescasseroli and the upper Sangro to exit from the condition of precariousness and impoverishment to which the decline of transhumance, the earthquake of Marsica, and World War I had confined them, imagining for them a future of redemption. It is also indubitable that without a figure like Erminio Sipari, his authority, his political capacity, and, above all, his steadfast determination, the peculiarities of this land, the rugged orography, or the centuries-old isolation would not have been enough to give us this heritage of nature and culture that is our Abruzzo Park.

Bibliography

Alberti Leandro. 1550. *Descrittione di tutta Italia, nella quale si contiene il sito di essa, l'origine et le Signorie delle Città et delle Castella.* Bologna: Giaccarello.

Altobello, Giuseppe .1921. *Fauna dell'Abruzzo e del Molise. Mammiferi. IV. I Carnivori (Carnivora).* Campobasso: Casa Tipografico-Editrice Colitti.

Arnone Sipari, Lorenzo. 1998. Dalla Riserva Reale dell'Alta Val di Sangro alla costituzione del Parco Nazionale d'Abruzzo. In Emiliano Giancristofaro (ed.), *La lunga guerra per il Parco Nazionale d'Abruzzo*, 49-66. Lanciano: Rivista Abruzzese.

Arnone Sipari, Lorenzo (ed.). 2011. *Scritti scelti di Erminio Sipari sul Parco Nazionale d'Abruzzo (1922-1933).* Trento: Temi.

Balzano, Vincenzo. 1935. *Documenti per la storia di Castel di Sangro, vol. III.* L'Aquila: Vecchioni.

D'Andrea, Uberto. 1981. *Notizie storiche su l'Alto Sangro e l'Alto Molise, vol. I.* Casamari: Tipografia dell'Abbazia.

Felice, Costantino. 2009. Le *trappole dell'identità: l'Abruzzo, le catastrofi, l'Italia di oggi.* Rome: Donzelli.

Guacci, Corradino. 1995. *Giuseppe Altobello naturalista molisano.* Isernia: Marinelli.

Mascilli Migliorini, Luigi (ed.). 1994. *La caccia al tempo dei Borbone.* Florence: Vallecchi.

Pedrotti, Franco. 1988. *Alle origini del Parco nazionale d'Abruzzo: le iniziative di Pietro Romualdo Pirotta.* Camerino: Università di Camerino.

Piccioni, Luigi. 1996. "Il dono dell'orso". Abitanti e plantigradi dell'Alta Val di Sangro tra Otto e Novecento. *Abruzzo contemporaneo* s. II n. 2: 61-113.

—. 1998. Una visione in anticipo sui tempi. L'intreccio tutela ambientale-sviluppo turistico alle origini del Parco Nazionale d'Abruzzo. In Emiliano Giancristofaro (ed.), *La lunga guerra per il Parco Nazionale d'Abruzzo*, 19-47. Lanciano: Rivista Abruzzese.

Sipari, Erminio. 1924. Il Parco Nazionale d'Abruzzo. *Nuova Antologia* 1256: 97-113.

—. 1926. *Relazione del Presidente del Direttorio provvisorio dell'Ente Autonomo del Parco Nazionale d'Abruzzo alla Commissione Amministratrice dell'Ente stesso, nominata con Regio Decreto 25 marzo 1923.* Tivoli: Maiella.

Vaccari, Lino. 1912. *Per la protezione della fauna italiana.* Tivoli: Maiella.

Vincenti, Pietro. 1604. *Historia della famiglia Cantelma composta dal dottore Pietro Vincenti della citta d'Hostuni.* Naples: Sottile.

SESSION II:

THE NATIONAL PARKS
OF THE NEIGHBOURING COUNTRIES

THE SWISS NATIONAL PARK AND THE INTERNATIONALISATION OF THE ENVIRONMENTAL ISSUES AT THE BEGINNING OF THE XXTH CENTURY

FRANÇOIS WALTER

Modern Switzerland was born in 1848 with the foundation of the Federal State, following a weak and rather archaic form of Confederation, in which the totally autonomous cantons jealously held their own sovereignty. Once invented Switzerland, however, the Swiss had to be created! In effect, it is not enough to have a delimited and structured state in order for the population living there to share the feeling of being a "nation", that is a community gathered in one land. All the second half of the nineteenth century is occupied by the efforts to build the Swiss identity, to reinforce the sense of belonging that is not exclusively local or cantonal. The Swiss have to learn to move mentally on another level, the federal or super-cantonal one. It is true, this process already started before 1848, because nationalism belongs, on the one hand, to the liberal ambition, and on the other hand has its roots in the eighteenth century "helvetism". Like in other European countries, the national culture needs an ideology that in turn legitimises its own existence, represents it through texts, metaphors, figurative expedients, images, and landscapes. The creation–relatively early for the European average–of a national park in 1914 cannot be understood if this context is not considered (Piccioni 2011, ed.).

The national ideology

Historians were largely mobilised to give legitimacy to some kind of origin and to support consequently a targeted idea of time: History is necessary to explain the present. All historical writing finds its focal point in the 1848 Constitution, result of a slow and organic construction. This kind of conception, emphasising the work of nineteenth-century Liberals, those who in Switzerland are called Radicals, holds a strong ideological nature. The radical ideologists were pleased to idealise the old Switzerland transforming it into "the oldest democracy of the World", of which the confederal State would be the organic development. In the future this myth will be accurately reproduced. Commentators insist on the exceptional existence (*historische Sonderexistenz*) of the country. According to them, the confederal State is not founded on race, community blood bonds, language or history. Unlike the great European powers, Switzerland will be born from a political "idea", a thought and a will. In effect, for the Swiss–attracted by the ethnic communities surrounding them to the North, South and East–nature, language, blood, and race are centrifugal forces; what founds the social bond is first of all the "certainty of being a better State under many aspects, of being a nationality that goes beyond the simple affinities of blood and language". The "history-making" historians who dominate the historiographical situation until the mid-twentieth century will repeat that some aspects of Swiss history have the feature of a *Sonderfall* that is a particular case. This canonical expression of the Swiss political culture is none other than the lay version of another certainty, ancient but ever alive, that Switzerland is a God-chosen country (Walter 2010, pp. 71-80).

The consolidation of the national ideology, however, needs solid points of reference, for this reason some places encapsulate the features of the nation's existence. The close symbiosis between nature and history is embodied by the site of the meadow of the Rütli (Grütli, in French), on Lake Lucerne. In the mid-nineteenth century this meadow physically becomes the sacred place where it is believed the events of the foundation of the nation were held. After becoming a national property, at the beginning of the 1860s, it has to be rearranged to fulfil its new symbolic functions. Landscape experts and architects of the École Polytechnique Fédérale are in charge of re-shaping a rural space, degraded by illegal pasturage, and elevate it to a place of memory. The massive planting of conifers, the zigzag paths, the construction of a cavern with blocks of limestone shipped by lake, the building of vernacular houses and a pier decorated with geraniums contribute to create the garden-landscape of the Swiss nation.

In Bern, the house of government and Parliament, called Palais Federal, was built in different stages. The administrative complex that we know today was finished at the end of the nineteenth century having become the object of an iconographic patriotic program, so that the central building represents a real book of images. To decorate the great hall of Parliament the Grütli is chosen instead of a historical scene. An artist from

Geneva, Charles Giron, paints this mythical landscape, a fresco of 12 meters by 6 representing the "cradle" of Swiss history.

The "true Switzerland", moreover, cannot be anything but mountainous. So, all Swiss history is re-interpreted in the light of a peculiar historical and topographic imagination. Shepherds and mountains become elements of the Swiss identity, as shown by Heidi, the heroine of Johanna Spyri's novels (1880-1881). In comparison with the great national states, Switzerland finds its legitimacy in its role as mother of the rivers *(Helvetia mater fluviorum)* and guardian of the mountain passes lying at the heart of Europe. Nature and landscape preservation, a typical sensitivity of the early twentieth century, promotes the patriotic image of the mountain threatened by railways and tourist facilities. The Swiss political conscience loves expressing itself through alpine references, so that it is not surprising that the work of Ferdinand Hodler (1853-1918), who stands out as a kind of official painter despite a figurative boldness often misunderstood by his contemporaries, deals with the subject of the Alps and Swiss history.

The logic of the *Heimatschutz*

Stressing the dangers for the environment does not yet develop in a real ecological approach in the current meaning of the term, rather in an awakening of a fundamentally aesthetic nostalgia for the harmony of nature. The new attention addressed to the damage caused by industrial and urban civilization certainly implies a change of approach toward nature, which can assume two forms: what is natural has to be both a useful and an aesthetic model. Here enters the concept–especially rich in symbolic implications–of *Heimatschutz*, a word coined by the German preservationist Ernst Rudorff in the 1880s.

When in 1909 the first international congress on the preservation of landscapes is held in Paris, Charles Beauquier, president of the Société des paysages de France (established in 1901), who organises the meeting, announces his debt to *Heimatschutz*. He explains that the German movement does not want to protect the fatherland (*Vaterland)* but rather the small homeland (*Heimat*), that is what in French should be defined as the "motherland, if we wish to coin a neologism that corresponds better to the warm and tender feelings that we feel towards our small homeland" (de Clermont 1910, ed., p. 12). At the beginning, it is also explained to us that the German members intend to safeguard "everything representing the national and peculiar character of the provinces: habits, traditions, plants and animals that tend to disappear and whose disappearance should be avoided". Under a lyrical impulse, an inspector from the Administration des Eaux et Forêts (Water and Forests Administration) defines even the heritage ideal of the beautiful French landscape: "At the highest level of the elements of beauty and artistic value of the landscape should be placed the forests which sometimes form a delicate ornament or contribute to the impressive view of our mountains together with the water of the creeks, the bubble of the falls and the wild slopes, sometimes make up the graceful places of our plains with the delicate banks of our streams or the quiet shores of our lakes, and sometimes are marked by a religious mystery thanks to the unique majesty of their high forests that seem to correspond–in this assortment of infinitely variegated aspects–to every tormented or peaceful, sad or merry secluded or inspired state of human thought" (de Clermont 1910, ed., p. 109). On his part, the German lecturer makes the exegesis of the word *Heimatschutz* that expresses in his opinion the "pious preservation of the original qualities belonging to every regime, so that this respect of the image of the country contributes to develop and preserve localism, bedrock of patriotic feeling". Then he adds: "What is especially necessary to safeguard is the image of the Homeland, whether delightful or severe: its beloved borders must be respected by everyone". And this against the extravagances of capitalism and Americanism (de Clermont 1910, ed., p. 109).

During this kind of meeting, the preservation of places is widely debated as is the comparison of the first laws that in many countries oppose publicity–perceived as a symbol of consumer society–through the regulation of billposting (in Prussia and Great Britain in 1907, in France and Belgium in 1909). This approach substitutes and prolongs the preceding tendency towards the protection of the artistic and architectonic heritage. The sensitization towards historical monuments established itself at the time of the French Revolution, when the most far-sighted people stand up against the destructive vandalism of the symbols of the defeated monarchy. There will be a series of measures aimed at protecting the historical and artistic heritage. For this reason the notion of historical monument dates back to 1790 (Quatremère de Quincy, Lenoir, etc). The Commission des Monuments Historiques is born in 1834, while later there will be the founding laws of the heritage policy: in France that of March, 30 1887, in Italy that of June, 20 1909.

What characterises the nineteenth century is a first extension of this logic of heritage that also tends to absorb objects of nature. The selection of the objects to redefine to invent the heritage is not obvious. At which level is it necessary to act? Must the object be outlined in space or have a variable perimeter? Is it possible to conciliate cultural and natural values? Even if the polygraph and great traveller Alexander Humboldt has already talked in 1814 about "natural monuments" *(Naturdenkmal)* and even if from the mid-nineteenth century here and there some rocky formations and natural curiosities have been protected, it is only toward the twentieth century that the constitution of "reliquary" landscapes and the transformation of landscapes into museums become social practices and national values.

Aesthetical contemplation remains central in the relationship with nature typical of the Belle Époque. In Switzerland the initiator of the *Heimatschutz* is the poetess and painter Marguerite Burnat-Provins who became well-known thanks to a series of newspaper articles published in March 1905 with a shocking title: "The Cancers". On the first page of a daily newspaper she expresses her fear of the plague that threatens our landscapes: "Why this insult to the eternal beauty of the mountains? Why this smack to such a noble nature, whose only duty seemed to emanate charm?" Thus, it is no longer enough to invent and become accustomed to a contemplative perception, but it is necessary to struggle to safeguard the same objects that provoke emotion. The passage is from contemplation to protective action: "Trees fall–she writes–the bridled creeks are used for the most obscene matters, the wounds on the side of the mountains get wider. On the cruelly flattened lands shapeless buildings are erected in pustolous clusters, horror spreads where grace once ruled". After numerous encouraging reactions caused by her first article Marguerite Burnat-Provins proposes, on March 29, 1905, to launch "an extended and fraternal association against vandalism" named Ligue pour la beauté. Later she will explain that, in her opinion, it was about reacting to landscape "prostitution" because emotion before aesthetic values embodied by a landscape represents a vital need (*Gazette de Lausanne,* March, 17 and 29 1905).

The initiative has an immediate success and soon, in July 1905, an association recruiting members from all over Switzerland is constituted. It is the Schweizerische Vereinigung für Heimatschutz, Swiss variation of the German Schweizerische Vereinigung für Heimatschutz, founded in Dresden in 1904. In French it becomes the Ligue pour la conservation de la Suisse pictoresque because the word *Heimatschutz* is impossible to translate. Switzerland, the first militant, seems condemned to become banal just when it embodies the ideal of picturesque and banality is "what we see everywhere, what looks like everything". At the beginning the Ligue is mobilised against the project of the Matterhorn railway, a track to be installed on the North-East side whose access to the peak would be guaranteed by an underground funicular railway inside the famous rocky pyramid. The association became famous also for its continuous complaint about the "Americanism" that is expressed especially through the proliferation of posters and advertisements (Walter 1990, pp. 114-132).

The environmental element of the *Heimatschutz* ideology

Like everywhere in Europe, also in Switzerland the different scientific societies are worried about the safeguard of the heritage. Protected objects best illustrate the assimilation of homeland and landscape. For this reason, for example, the disappearance of centuries-old trees, witnesses of past historical events, moves us. The progress of glaciology lends a fascinating nature to the erratic boulders, these granite or gneiss fragments that scatter the plains and that are witnesses, as has been understood since the 1840s, of the Quaternary advance of glaciers. In 1867, the Commission Géologique Suisse launched an appeal "to the Swiss for the purpose of preserving erratic boulders", witnesses of the historical upheaval of the national landscape. Hundreds of them are inventoried and represented in cartographies so that they do not end up under the picks of the quarrymen or the producers of construction materials. Some patrons collect boulders to give to the scientific societies. The movement, however, deals also with plants, whose fragile alpine flowers seem to best embody the quintessence of Helvetia, a small nation in a hostile context of great countries that affirm their imperial ambitions. The edelweiss, for example, that has a strong symbolic connotation, will be protected from 1878.

The extension of the concept of monument, originally greatly limited, to a more extended environmental space begins in the German context (Walter 2004). At the beginning of the twentieth century the notion finds an effective appeal. A founding role has been rightly attributed a posteriori to the small book of the botanist Hugo Conwentz (1855-1922) re-published ceaselessly from its first edition in 1904. Initially it was a report intended to inform the minister of Culture, Education and Health of the conservationist issue; in volume-form, it has become the reference for supporters of nature protection. In it, the author expresses his certainty about the need for immediate action to avoid the complete destruction of primitive nature (Conwentz 1904). Just as we are used to considering a menhir or a tumulus historical monuments, it is now necessary to admit that the erratic boulder and the mountain formation represent monuments of nature. But there is more than that. A natural landscape in its totality, with its form, its streams, its lakes, its plant and animal communities can aspire to the level of natural monument in the same way as the rare species of the original flora and fauna.

The dangers threatening natural monuments are different. The author recalls the disfigurement caused by tourism, the abuses of publicity and the collections that can make some vegetal and animal species disappear. Even if it is an ancient country of civilization, Italy would distinguish itself, according to Conwentz, for being an especially predatory nation, a topos that will last the entire twentieth century: the hunt would be the substitute of gymnastics and the destruction of song birds would become a sport. So Conwentz makes a list of the most endangered plants and animals, speaks out against the extermination of some species, stigmatizes the draining of the swamps, the lowering of water-bearing strata, indiscriminate farming, the rooting out of hedges, the super-exploitation of construction materials, points out how the forests pay a heavy toll for an excessive exploitation. The original forests are replaced by more profitable exotic essences to the detriment of the global aspect of the landscape and the faunal and floristic equilibrium. But the author also denounces the offences to the landscape provoked by industrial activities: noxious gases destroy the forests and especially the conifers, whose degradation in the Harz has already been observed in the mid-eighteenth century; surface waters are dirty, sometimes coloured, like around Dresden, where in summer they become red due to the dumping of zinc muds.

After this depressing picture of the state of what he considers to be the heritage of nature, Conwentz lists a series of concrete proposals. Conservation has to develop on three fronts: first of all, natural monuments have to be inventoried and mapped, then actions have to be taken to protect them "on the ground" and finally they have to be promoted. If Conwentz has already realized the inventory of the trees and vegetal formations of the Kingdom of Prussia (Conwentz 1900), here he also alludes to the cartography of the habitat of the Swiss avifauna, Swedish falls and rapids, the most remarkable trees of Prussia or the glacial striations of Sweden and Finland. Regarding the second stage, protection, this is about immediately resolving the problem of the objects worthy of protection and guaranteeing "on the ground" their identification (a name, a distinctive mark, a way to outline them that can be integrated in the landscape). Finally, becoming conscious of the value of this heritage is to assure its safety. Conwentz gives crucial importance to the development of the teaching of the *Heimatkunde*, a hard to translate word that corresponds to the knowledge of the local environment by taking the example of Prussia, where the scholastic authorities have given great importance to the diffusion in schools of wall maps to teach prehistory, the publication of maps of extraordinary landscapes, shapes of mountains, animal and vegetal species, namely the many representations that make up the features of the "homeland face" (Conwentz 1904, pp. 127-28). But the author is alert to the numerous local initiatives aimed to safeguard fragments of landscape or famous sites. He mentions many German, Austrian, Russian, Danish, Italian, Belgian, Norwegian and British cases, without forgetting that of the Swiss meadows of Rütli, acquired again thanks to the young people in the mid-nineteenth century and made artistic in the form of a sacred landscape, cradle of Helvetic history (Walter 2004, pp. 340-41).

In effect, Conwentz deals mainly with woodland protection. He hopes that the impact studies be carried out in the forests where industrial facilities (quarries, sawmills, mines) or infrastructures (roads) have been installed. This kind of transformation has to be made so that "the beauty of landscape is damaged as little as possible" (Conwentz 1904, p. 146). The conservation of the wild state of marshy areas seems to be one of his main preoccupations. Our man knows very well the environment of Northern Germany and the Scandinavian countries: for him, this kind of landscape embodies true nature. He also wishes that the authorities in charge of controlling the colonisation projects in Prussia be more zealous in conserving the natural monuments and avoiding the complete uniformity of landscapes when any works of valorisation are undertaken.

The conclusion is explicit and inscribes the proposal in a political and patriotic context. According to the author it concerns locally protecting the territory of the small homeland, but in a wider sense also that of the whole German homeland. To protect natural monuments represents an undertaking of national interest, whose aim is the increase of joy and love of the native soil (Conwentz 1904, p. 207). Here we are at the heart of the fundamental homology between homeland and heritage.

After the publication of the handbook, in 1906 Conwentz is appointed to organise a state office for natural monuments protection (Staatliche Stelle für Naturdenkmalpflege in Preussen). Initially (1909) the institute is located in Gdańsk and after, in 1911, is moved to Berlin. However, the failed approval of a bill by the Prussian Parliament during 1912 reduces the task of the office to mere research and documentary activity. Conwentz increases his travels for studying, participates in great international congresses and conferences where naturalistic issues become popular thanks to the new apparatus of luminous projection.

The ideological mobilisation of the landscape as heritage corresponds in a certain measure to a twisting of these ideas and to a change of level in their field of application. In the period preceding the outbreak of the war, in effect, the antimodernist and nationalist propagandists rapidly take over the issue (Wettengel 1993, pp. 372 et seq.). Conwentz's over-rational positions are overtaken by the demagogy of new mass associations in which protectionist action becomes central, as in the case of the Bund für Naturschutz. The Prussian office is reproached for an over-fragmented vision of protection, a concept that is interested only in outlined objects when landscape degradation works on a global scale (Groud 2001, pp. 89-114). The intent is to oppose this fragmented and extemporaneous vision with a museographic concept of the German landscape as a whole, which integrates the forms of life and habits of the residents of this endangered space. Some people associate nature protection, defence of race and "struggle for the vital strength of the nation" (Hermann Löns in 1906), echoed by the regret of the Swiss theorist Georges de Montenach for the impossibility of establishing "local reserves where the ancient qualities of our race would be cultivated and safeguarded, like gorgeous alpine flowers" (Wettengel 1993, p. 373; Walter 1990, p. 136).

Global conservation in situ, on the other hand, has developed mainly in Sweden under the impulse of the ethnographer and philologist Artur Hazelius (1833-1901). From 1870 he systematically collected ethnographic objects and then opened his collections to the public founding the Nordiska Museet in 1880. Heritage, he says, has to stimulate "the patriotic feelings of the visitors" (Maure 1993). He extends the concept developing the scenography that requires the use of buildings and, obviously, of open spaces. The Swedish scholar establishes his museum on the Skansen hill (that is the Redpubt, from the name of the pre-existing fortification) in the royal park of Djurgården, in Stockholm. In this park defined by Hazelius as "historical and cultural" is the first open air museum of the world, initially in 1891 visitors can admire only a house recovered in the province of Dalarna, but slowly Hazelius expanded the property (today of about 300,000 square meters) to realise a "living museum" (Bancel 2002), where the representative buildings of vernacular architecture of the different Swedish regions are reproduced and also, what matters more, authentic inhabitants with their traditional costumes attending their traditional duties, at least according to the knowledge that we have, lived, offering to the visitors "national" dances and songs. Natural environment is reproduced as well, with its specific vegetation and fauna. In places where only sparse pines grew impressive works are necessary to bring fertile soil and transplant thousands of trees respecting a precise spatial division: the Lappish camp is in the northern part of the Skansen, while the Scania farm is in the southern one. Later the museum officials will make the effort of outlining also the forest areas, from the arctic birch wood to the most southern beech grove (Blent 2002, ed.).

From *Heimatschutz* to *Naturschutz*

At the end of the nineteenth century and at the beginning of the twentieth, the strengthening of the certainty that the moment has come to safeguard as much as possible form the "fury of destruction that possesses the modern world" (*Amtliches Stenographisches Bulletin der Schweizerischen Bundesversammlung*, 24, 1914, p. 161) obeys a museographic logic. It is the same climate with aesthetic leanings and full of nationalist ideology that presides over the creation of nature protection associations and the foundation of the Swiss National Park will be their great achievement. In my opinion, it is opportune to distinguish the property worries that contaminate the scientific societies interested in natural curiosities from the instrumental use of sociability at the service of a great idea led by some isolated figures of Swiss scientific circles. At the end of the nineteenth century and at the beginning of the following one, it is possible to see, on the other hand, an intense circulation of models and ideas. These exchanges are soon destined to give a transnational dimension to nature protection.

Let us start by remembering the prestige of the American model and references to the romantic natural philosophy of the return to nature already illustrated in the first half of the nineteenth century by the figures of Ralph Waldo Emerson and Henry David Thoreau. In 1864 the reserve in the Yosemite Valley and in 1872 the immense natural reserve of Yellowstone are created in the United States. These achievements were the object of an extraordinary popularity through the media and are recalled in German speaking Europe mainly thanks to Conwentz. Nevertheless the European situation is very different: in the United States nature is inevitably associated to wild and virgin spaces, defined by the word "wilderness", while in Europe nature can seldom be separated from the aesthetic, cultural, ethic and patriotic aspects established by the different nations. Even in Switzerland the mythical images of geysers, natural arches, canyons and immense forests obviously are not enough to allow the emergence of protectionist practices. However, the images are undoubtedly important and go together with a peculiar conjuncture of multiple actors: local administrations, federal authorities, pressure groups, scientific associations and, certainly, some personalities who know how to direct public opinion at the right moment and propose solutions.

So in April 1905 the town of Monthey, in the Valais, finds out that the granite boulder known with the name of Pierre-des-Marmettes will finish under the blows of the pick axe. The local authority is shocked and appeals to the new-born Ligue pour la beauté. Through Marguerite Burnat-

Provins' pen the organisation launches "a pressing appeal to the scientific world in order to support the local residents of the Valais who defend the venerable rock whose beauty they have understood". Simultaneously, the city council asks the Confederation to intervene. The Department of Home Affairs which does not have the infrastructures necessary for a nature protection policy, addresses with great embarrassment the Société helvétique des sciences naturelles (SHSN) and finally the boulder will be saved thanks to the united economic intervention of the municipality, the Confederation and the great scientific societies.

Based on this experience, the SHSN thus decides in 1906 to create a commission for nature protection (Schweizerische Naturschutzkommission, SNK). The final aim is to try to institutionalise protection, overcome the evident limits of public administrations and–why not?–obtain the establishment of an office similar to that directed by Conwentz in Prussia. The commission is composed of scientists (geologists, botanists, zoologists, palaeontologists, forest engineers and geographers) and is officially devoted to the protection of natural monuments, of "what yet exists of the fauna, flora, erratic boulders and documents of the prehistory that have been handed down as heritage through the centuries and that form part of the aesthetic and intellectual heritage of everyone loving their country" (*Journal forestier suisse*, January 1910, p. 14-16; see also Glutz 1905, p. 7 and 38). For the Commission nature is, in some way, a pure scientific curiosity. The disappearance of wild species is considered inescapable due to progress which is not brought into question, nor is the general economic evolution model. What prevails is, simply, a clearer perception of the antagonism between beauty of landscape and technologic infrastructures. The first president of the Commission is Paul Sarasin (1856-1929), a scholar from Basle with an education as doctor and zoologist, who will never become a university professor and will participate in many scientific expeditions to Ceylon and Celebes, whose reports–published in numerous volumes–will introduce him in the German ethnographic and naturalist circles.

The first proposal for a natural park was elaborated in 1906 in the Naturschutzkommission by a botany professor at the École Polytechnique Fédérale of Zürich, Carl Schröter, a member of the Commission, even if the idea had been circulating for quite some time: in fact, the matter is debated also in the forestry circles, where the previous year Robert Glutz had praised the achievement of forest reserves (*Urwald-Reservationen*). The Société de Physique et d'Histoire Naturelle of Geneva intervenes at the Federal Council in order that it realise some "geographic reserves" instead of continuing the railway project of the Matterhorn. The request cites explicitly "what has been done in the United States of America". The controversy over the Matterhorn project offers a favourable media context. The jurist Hermann Christ, an enthusiast of botany and member of the Commission, writes in a daily newspaper of Basel "here we are, it is the last hour: let us hurry to intervene in the direction long-requested, before the Matterhorn is vandalized" (Kupper 2012, p. 68). The Federal Council transmits the request from Geneva to the Société helvétique des sciences naturelles which in August 1907, replies that an ad hoc commission is already studying the modification to establish a reserve.

In 1907 the Commission is initially interested in the site of St. Peter's Island but soon establishes that it is a *Kulturlandschaft* (anthropized space) greatly lacking in biodiversity. The following year the Commission visits the Grisons with the botanist Steivan Brunies, future secretary of the League, who directs attention towards the advantages of the Val Cluozza, an almost intact place. Thanks to an intense lobbying activity, the SNK receives from the Confederation a sort of unofficial mandate to proceed. The project is conducted by a sub-commission directed by Paul Sarasin together with his cousin Fritz (at that time president of the SHSN), Carl Schröter and the zoologist Friedrich Zschokke, all from Basel and members of the Club Alpin Suisse. One of the most brilliant intuitions of the group is to create in parallel, as an extension of its activity, a structure of popular fundraising. In 1909, in fact, the SHSN organises the Swiss League for Nature Protection (Schweizerischer Bund für Naturschutz, today known as Pro Natura, name adopted in 1997) and Paul Sarasin is its first president. The subscription of a franc a year is accessible to a vast public wishing to contribute to protect what is proposed to them as the "Urnatur", that is the original nature of the homeland. In 1912 the League will count 20.000 members.

Thus it is in the Alps, in the lower Engadine (Canton of Grisons) and more precisely in the Val Cluozza that the Swiss National Park is finally created in 1914. The official request of financing from the Confederation is deposited in 1911 and federal support is guaranteed by the approval of a parliamentary provision which symbolically enters in force on August, 1 1914, a national holiday. Fate would have it that the decision was taken before the outbreak of the war, otherwise the foundation of the Park would have certainly been postponed. Article 1 of the Law says: "It is established a national park outlined through contract and belonging to the town of Zernez. All the animals and plants included within this territory *will be totally left to their natural development* and subtracted from any human influence that is practised outside the aims pursued by the creation of the Park. The National Park will be the object of scientific observations"

("Feuille fédérale suisse", no. 51, December, 18 1912, p. 445-455). In 1914 the Société Suisse des Sciences Naturelles can already be proud of having obtained a *nationales Naturheiligtum*, a national sanctuary (Kupper 2012, p. 75).

The transnational dimension

The enemies of the institution do not fail to point out the risks of allowing nature to develop freely, a focus for the proliferation of parasitic insects and wild animals dangerous for the rest of the territory. The supporters of the park reply to this fear of return to the wild by saying it will be the game of natural balance that will avoid such an evolution fore-shadowing ideas closer to our concept of ecosystem. But what favours the consensus of the members of Parliament more than anything else is the need to protect nature from the "fury of destruction that possesses the modern world", to use the words of the francophone report of 1914 of the National Council Commission. More prosaically, other opponents do not fail to observe that situating the park in a border zone would offer a juicy opportunity to Italian poachers!

The circulation of models

The first surprising element is that the choice of the area sets the Park in an alpine region lacking in remarkable peaks, particularly magnificent landscapes, exceptional natural curiosities, glaciers or waterfalls. Thus we are in the presence of something opposed to the *spectacular* that founds American-style conservation. Using a classically comparative method it is certainly necessary to observe that the American park and the Swiss park are antinomic models, if we consider that up to this stage of planning the reference to the north-American achievements had been constant.

First of all, the dimensions are not comparable: the 170 square kilometres against the 3,300 square miles of Yellowstone! The American parks benefit from state protection while the Swiss park remains a private enterprise even if financed by the State. In the United States the protected areas are perceived as huge gardens or places for recreation (bathing in the geysers is allowed) while in Switzerland there is rigid protection and strictly regulated access for scientific reasons, that is to procure a privileged research ground for naturalists. On one side the will is to protect the last vestiges of virgin nature threatened by civilisation while on the other side, in Engadine, they try to create the conditions allowing the reproduction of wildlife "as it was before the appearance of man", to use the eloquent expression of Paul Sarasin (Walter 1990, p. 122; Schröter 1918, pp. 761-65). In his remarkable study on the history of the Swiss park, Patrick Kupper analysed the ways of translating the models (Kupper 2012), observing how at the beginning of the twentieth century the idea that the first national park had been achieved in the United States was already widespread, seeing in that the production of a real myth. Even if in Switzerland the word "reserve" (*Reservation* in German) was used for a long time, the expression "national park" seems to impose itself around 1910 because, according to Kupper the American expression seems more seductive but also because, as is deduced from the texts, the German word *Reservation* which refers to wild nature is not easy to translate in French or Italian. In Germany, where anti-Americanism seems relatively widespread, the expression "national park" is absolutely avoided and the traditional one of *Naturschutzpark*, that is natural protected park is preferred. Sweden from its point of view presents an interesting case (Mels 1999) because its first "national" parks are dated 1909: the park of Abisko in the North of the country extends over 7.700 hectares while the park of Ängsö, near Stockholm, only 168 hectares. The legal bases of these reserves are quite ambivalent because the law on natural monuments protection is clearly restrictive and patrimonial, while the law on national parks recalls the concept of public leisure park following the American model. In general it is possible to affirm that in Europe the expression "national park" is used when the reference model is the Swiss park, which is, on the contrary, an integral reserve, a true anti-model compared to the American one (Hall 1929, p. 669). For the historian it is a great example of the circulation of models and at the same time of phenomena of appropriation of references and concepts in different contexts acting as very distinct social uses.

The opening to world protection

It is necessary to underline another dimension, in this case very peculiar: the opening to planetary nature protection. It matured during the great international congresses that at the end of the nineteenth century gather together scientists from different disciplines. At the time of the first international congress of ornithologists, in 1884, it seems clear that bird protection can advance only thanks to international solutions with the cooperation of the different States. The internationalisation of environmental issues owes a lot to the figure of Paul Sarasin. During his journeys to Asia Sarasin became aware of the risks that frantic exploitation of resources in colonial countries meant for the environment. It is thus in the framework of the great international zoology congresses, and especially in the third held in Graz in 1910, that he expresses his preoccupations suggesting "to extend nature protection to the whole Earth, from the North Pole to the South Pole, both on dry land and in the sea" (Conference de Berne 1914, p. 23). His colleagues consequently give him the task of creating a worldwide commission for nature protection, asking him to undertake all the necessary steps "through the Swiss Federal Council". Recurring to a neutral country is a consolidated praxis in the context of increasing imperial rivalries: Switzerland, not having any colonial possessions, seems the most suitable for mediating in the case of conflicts. On the other hand, this kind of intervention corresponds quite well with the political interests of this small country, which is excluded from big international debates due to its neutrality but at the same time aspires to occupy a seat in the orchestra of nations. Lacking the political-military weight of the great powers, Switzerland expresses itself on the one hand through the extension of its economic network and on the other hand thanks to its diplomatic skills. Nature protection is one of the many sectors in which these skills can be displayed and so in Bern, in November 1913, the first international conference on nature conservation is held, with the aim of laying the foundations for a global achievement. The first worry of the delegates of the seventeen nations represented in Bern, including France, Germany, Italy, Russia and Austria-Hungary is the massacre of cetaceous and seals and threatened fauna of the Arctic and Antarctic regions. The representatives are worried by the diminishing of the fur animals in Russia, Canada and the United States. The South-American chinchilla, the European beaver, the bison, the African big game represent the object of circumstantial relations, without forgetting in this list "the most beautiful" among the tasks that fall to world nature protection, that of "saving from extermination the last primitive populations and conserving them as intact as possible".

What counts concerning our issue is that since its genesis the project of a national park in Switzerland has been inscribed in a transnational dimension. The botanist Steivan Brunies is sure about this when he points out, in 1914, that due to its location on the Italian and Austro-Hungarian borders the park of Grigions anticipates in a certain sense the international cooperation that is extending nature conservation all over the world, from one Pole to the other. (Kupper 2012, p. 88).

However, according to the analysis of the German historian Anna-Katharina Wöbse, the greatest specialist today on these matters, it is important to remember that–considering the contexts we have cited from the beginning–the choice of internationalisation was not taken for granted

(Wöbse 2012). It can be perceived from the stance taken by different scientists, like the Russian zoologist Kozhevnikov who in 1907 develops a holistic view of the protection of spaces where human intervention is banned for scientific reasons (Wöbse 2006, p. 630), but the theorists of protection and heritage preservation like Hugo Conwentz affirm, on the contrary, some solutions of a national type. The moment of glory of the latter is surely the first international congress for landscapes protection held in Paris in 1909 where he was the most prominent figure; here he illustrates the field of activity of the *Heimatschutz*, the admired Prussian model (de Clermont 1910, ed.). But then, at the congress of Bern in 1913, Conwentz will be the only one to sustain nature conservation as a strictly national duty, opposing Paul Sarasin's project of giving to a super-national commission the task of dictating the norms and monitoring their application. Sarasin imagined in fact not only building a network of great protected areas, of "intangible sanctuaries" (*unantastbare Sanktuarien*) but also to give to a world commission for nature protection (*Weltnaturschutzkommission*) the mission of creating these reserves "everywhere on the globe, from Pole to Pole" in order to "internationalise" the issue (Sarasin 1914, pp. 38-39). The German model, on the other hand, is linked to the Swiss one in its modalities of conservation, very strict and with mainly scientific aims. The German theorist thus shares in Sarasin's resistance to following the American model and its touristic aims and in contesting the American claim of working as a universal model. Paralysed by the war, this international dimension will take a long time to bloom again, but this is not the place to tell its story.

Bibliography

Bancel, Nicolas (ed.). 2002. *Zoos humains XIXe et XXe siècles, de la Vénus hottentote aux reality shows*. Paris: La Découverte.

Blent, Karin (ed.). 2002. *Skansen*. Uppsala: Ord & Form AB.

de Clermont, Raoul (ed.). 1910. *Le Ier Congrès International pour la protection des paysages (Paris, October, 17-20 1909)*. Paris: Société pour la protection des paysages de France.

Conference de Berne. 1914. *Recueil des Procès-verbaux de la Conférence internationale pour la protection de la Nature, Berne November, 7-19 1913*. Berne: K. J. Wyss.

Conwentz. Hugo.1900. *Forstbotanisches Merkbuch. Nachweis der beachtenswerten und zu schützenden urwüchsigen Sträucher, Bäume und Bestände im Königreich Preußen*. Berlin: Borntraeger.

—. 1904. *Die Gefährdung der Naturdenkmäler und Vorschläge zu ihrer Erhaltung. Denkschrift, dem Herrn Minister der geistlichen, Unterrichts- und Medizinal-Angelegenheiten überreicht.* Berlin: Borntraeger.

Glutz, Robert. 1905. *Ueber Natur-Denkmäler, ihre Gefährdung und Erhaltung.* Solothurn: Union.

Groud, Hervé. 2001. Le paysage et le droit. *Travaux de l'Institut de Géographie de Reims* 105-106: 89-114.

Hall, Harvey M.1929. European Reservations for the Protection of Natural Conditions. *Journal of Forestry* 6: 667-684.

Kupper, Patrick. 2012. *Wildnis schaffen. Eine transnationale Geschichte des Schweizerischen Nationalparks.* Bern: Haupt.

Maure, Marc. 1993. Nation, paysan et musée. La naissance des musées d'ethnographie dans les pays scandinaves (1870-1904). *Terrain* 20.

Mels, Tom. 1999. *Wild Landscapes. The Cultural Nature of Swedish National Parks.* Lund: Lund University Press.

Piccioni, Luigi (ed.). 2011. *Cento anni di parchi nazionali in Europa e in Italia.* Pisa: ETS.

Sarasin, Paul. 1914. *Ueber die Aufgaben des Weltnaturschutzes. Denkschrift gelesen an der Delegiertenversammlung zur Weltnaturschutzkommission in Bern am 18. November 1913.* Basel: Helbing & Lichtenhahn.

Schröter, Carl. 1918. Der schweizerische Nationalpark im Unterengadin. *Die Naturwissenschaften* 52: 761-765.

Walter, François. 1990. *Les Suisses et l'environnement. Une histoire du rapport à la nature du 18e siècle à nos jours.* Geneva: Ed. Zoé.

—. 2004. *Les figures paysagères de la nation. Territoire et paysage en Europe (16e-20e siècle).* Paris: Éditions de l'EHESS.

—. 2010. *Histoire de la Suisse. IV. La création de la Suisse moderne (1830-1930).* Neuchâtel: Alphil.

Wettengel, Michael. 1993. Staat und Naturschutz 1906-1945. Zur Geschichte der Staatlichen Stelle für Naturdenkmalpflege in Preußen und der Reichsstelle für Naturschutz. *Historische Zeitschrift* 257: 355-99.

Wöbse, Anna-Katharina. 2006. Naturschutz global- oder : Hilfe von außen. Internationale Beziehungen des amtlichen Naturschutzes im 20. Jahrhundert. In Bundesamt für Naturschutz (ed.), *Natur und Staat. Staatlicher Naturschutz in Deutschland 1906-2006.* Bonn: Bundesamt für Naturschutz.

—. 2012. *Weltnaturschutz. Umweltdiplomatie in Völkerbund und Vereinten Nationen 1920-1950.* Frankfurt: Campus Verlag.

THE GENESIS OF FRENCH NATIONAL PARKS

HENRI JAFFEUX

At the end of the nineteenth century, whilst the idea of national parks is blossoming in the New World, neither a similar official definition nor any legislation is forthcoming in France. The concept will gradually develop through numerous international meetings after the first American achievements. For some countries, such as France, Great Britain and Belgium, the first achievements will be realised, between the two World Wars, in the colonial dominions where the context is comparable to that of the so-called "new nations".

In Europe, the movement is launched shortly before World War I. In 1906, on the initiative of professor Hugo Conwentz the German empire equips itself with a central office for nature protection, whose role is to carry out research and propose the creation of nature reserves. However, the first European national parks are established in 1909 in Sweden with the creation of the Lapland parks (Sarek and Stora Sjöfallet), and in 1914 in Switzerland (Engadine). Other parks will follow after the war: 1918 in Spain (Covadonga, Ordesa), yourselves here in Abruzzo, then Gran Paradiso in 1922, in Poland in 1936, etc.

And France?

France does not remain passive, even if it must be said that any actual achievements will take longer to realise than in other European countries. This delay will last until the passing of the bill in 1960 even if some premonitory signs of this awareness in favour of heritage protection, then understood as historical monuments, aesthetics and landscape beauty, can be found as of the nineteenth century and the early years of the twentieth. The first attempts at protection in the forest of Fontainebleau, the founding of the Société de Protection des Paysages de France in 1901, the Beauquier bill for the "protection of natural sites and monuments of artistic character" of 1906 and the fact that the first international congress for the protection of landscapes was held in Paris in 1909, all eloquently demonstrate that our nation did not stay on the side lines of the dawning movement.

At the turn of the nineteenth century, even the matter of national parks is echoed in France by numerous technicians and forestry officials and the urban élite, particularly those who belong to the Club Alpin Français, the Touring Club de France, the Société pour la protection des Paysages de France and many of the scientific societies scattered over national territory. From 1902, these associations undertake the realisation of a national park of Esterel and they do not cease to take initiatives and to try to convince politicians of the need to protect sites and scenery of national importance. However, the majority of politicians, apparently paralysed by the thought of bringing property rights under discussion, refuse to commit themselves.

The question of protecting or managing and enhancing territories soon encourages public debate. This is well illustrated by the determined action of a prominent figure of these years, the member of Parliament for Doubs, Charles Beauquier (1833-1916), one of the rare contemporary politicians to invest in this battle of ideas. In 1899, when the source and waterfall of the Lison stream, situated in his district, are threatened by a project for a pressure water pipe to produce electricity, Beauquier fights, to the detriment of the owner's private interests, for their protection. Convinced of the justice of this battle, from 1901, Beauquier proposes a parliamentary bill to organise the protection of natural sites and monuments. His obstinacy allows him to overcome opposition and leads to the adoption, five years later on April 21, 1906, of the law which carries his name. However, the supporters of national parks remain disappointed in that the parliamentary passage does not foresee their inclusion, even if this was the aim at the heart of the debate.

It is impossible to recall this period and these first attempts at protection without remembering the creation, on the part of the Ligue Française pour la Protection des Oiseaux, in 1912 of the first French ornithological reserve in Brittany. Everyone has their anniversaries and this year we celebrate at the same time the Ligue Française pour la Protection des Oiseaux, and the ornithological reserve of the Sept-Iles.

1913, the year of every hope

1913 is certainly the richest year for every sort of enterprise in favour of the creation of national parks. In June, on the initiative of the Touring Club, the first international forest congress is held in Paris in favour of the creation and extension of national parks in every country. In fact, to spread and better demonstrate their discussions, the congress members move to the alpine valley of Haut-Vénéon, the site chosen to establish the "first French national park".

The day after taking this stand–and thanks again to the Touring Club de France–the Association des Parcs Nationaux de France et des Colonies is created. Its first enterprise will be to support the efforts to establish and run this park, desired above all by Alphonse Mathey (1862-1927), curator of the Eaux et Forêts (Waters and Forests) of Grenoble.

Thanks to the efforts of another key character of this period, the initiator of the Swiss National Park, Paul Sarasin (1856-1929), the first international conference for the protection of nature organised by the Commission Suisse pour la Protection de la Nature, directed by Sarasin, is held in Bern in 1913. This meeting preannounces, alongside the forest conference in Paris, the beginning of a process which will spread throughout the twentieth century: the internationalisation of nature protection.

In the same year, at the request of the Club Alpin Français, always active in this respect, the great traveller and initiator of French speleology Edouard-Albert Martel (1859-1938) publishes a study into national parks in the world in which a definition is given and it ends with a call to review the Beauquier law of April 21, 1906 in such a way as to include the possibility of founding national parks. The following year the departmental commission of the Seine-et-Marne sites expresses a vote for creating a national park in the forest of Fontainebleau but the war brutally stops all these promising initiatives, both national and international and they will be taken up again only after the war.

The period between the two wars: the colonial parks episode

If after and due to the war the movement for creating national parks meets some difficulty in re-forming in metropolitan France, and if the national parks "attempted" , in effect more virtual than real, remain without a statute, between the two World Wars the initiatives and efforts in favour of creating parks and reserves in the French colonies multiply. Up to the moment of the proclamations of independence, in the sixties, their establishment in Algeria, Morocco, Madagascar, French Equatorial and Western Africa, were in fact numerous and varied.

The twelve national parks and seventeen integral reserves listed in the *Atlas des Réserves Naturelles dans le monde* published by the UICN in 1956 cover nearly 41,000 sq. kilometres that is, double our Amazonian national park in Guyana (20,300 sq. kilometres of central zone). Albeit important, this figure must be compared with the vastness of French colonial territories that were involved, they covered over eleven million square kilometres; these reserves represented only 0.4% which reached 1.2% if the 90,000 sq. kilometres of wildlife reserves were added.

Towards "national parks of silence"?

If in the period between the two World Wars the movement obtains significant results in the colonies, the attempts to create true national parks make a mark on metropolitan territory.

The National Park of Bérarde of 1913 becomes the National Park of Oisans, then Pelvoux in 1923 not without some difficulty being encountered by the forest officials in making it acceptable to the local populations. And it remains without an official statute.

Another two initiatives emerge but they soon flounder. The first concerns mount Caroux, in Hérault, and it is begun by the keeper of forests Jean Prioton (1898-1985) but after numerous postponements the project will be finally abandoned. The second concerns the massif of Vercors.

Alphonse Mathey, the founder of the Bérarde Park, in service in Grenoble, launches the first land purchases in the hopes of realising a national park on the Hauts-Plateaux In 1939 the Administration of Eaux et Forêts, la Société Nationale d'Acclimatation, the senators of Isère et Drôme obtain State intervention, but the war breaks out and this project flounders too.

In these years, other noteworthy initiatives are owed to the associative movement in general and in particular the Société Nationale d'Acclimatation de France (SNAF), at the origin of national parks later to be founded. Thanks to a policy of management conventions with town councils and private individuals, the Société Nationale d'Acclimatation succeeds in creating several "natural reserves" ahead of its time. This is the case regarding the creation in 1927 of the *réserve zoologique et botanique* of the Camargue, the natural reserve of Néouvielle in the Hautes-Pyrénées in 1935 and the reserve of Lauzanier in the Alps of Haute Provence. Like the outlines of national parks attempted in the same years these reserves do not have a legal status, but it is also true that their existence does not cause dispute. However, things will go differently when the Société Nationale d'Acclimatation tries to transform the Camargue reserve into a national park or when, much later, it will take into account the matter of the perimeters of the national parks of Ecrins, the Pyrenees and Mercantour, which will be created starting from these old reserves.

If "on the ground"–at least in metropolitan France–nature protection remains rudimental, France can boast many international initiatives which will lead, after World War II, to the creation of the Union Internationale pour la Protection de la Nature.

In 1923, ten years after the Berne conference, la Société d'Acclimatation, the Ligue pour la Protection des Oiseaux, and the Société pour la protection des Paysages organise the first international congress for the protection of nature and natural sites and monuments at the Museum of Natural History in Paris. In 1931 France will host another international congress on the same topic and at the same museum, organised this time by Professor Abel Gruvel (1870-1941).

Concerning the protection of natural sites and monuments of artistic character, it concludes that, albeit innovatory at the level of its principles, the 1906 law is limited at the level of application, allowing the protection of only certain picturesque sites and thereby in need of a movement to revise it. This target will be reached with the new law of May 2, 1930 which is "bold, in taking a stand on property rights ratifying that the property can be registered even without the owners' consent if general interest justifies this" and in this sense it fulfils the wish made by Victor Hugo... a century before. This great legal progress will be one of the foundation stones of the national parks law of thirty years later.

In 1932 the writer Georges Duhamel (1884-1966) publishes an essay destined to have some success entitled "Le Parc national du silence" Condemning modern civilisation, Duhamel yearns for an imaginary park: " a wide and pleasant region, intelligently silent, endowed with hotels, saved from railways, air routes, industry...".

In 1933 the Société Française de Biogéographie decides to carry out a survey and to reflect upon the "way in which the reserves and the national parks of the whole world have been understood and accomplished with the aim of deducing rules that will illuminate public powers concerning future measures to be taken". The research, launched at the beginning of the year with the collaboration of some twenty affirmed specialists (C. Bressou, P. Chouard, H. Humbert, L. Lavauden, G. Petit, P. Vayssière) is in part deprived of its theoretical and practical interest by the almost contemporary proceedings of the international conference for the protection of African fauna and flora held in London that October. Here, in effect, the people attending come to an agreement about definitions and include them in the Convention on conservation of fauna and flora in the natural state adopted on November 8. Nevertheless, the study by the Société Française de Biogéographie, published in 1937, still remains a major reference work for historians of natural parks and reserves.

To conclude this period we also need to observe how, during the thirties different directors and personalities of the Savoy hunting world, having seen the failure of all attempts to safeguard the ibex (*Capra ibex*) regulating hunting in the department, push for the creation of a territory in which the species can be protected. Numerous initiatives will follow this admission of failure to regulate and control hunting, starting with the same hunting circles so that a territory bordering your Gran Paradiso national park be defined and destined for protection. However, the debate flounders both on the way to define perimeters and on the statute to give to the territory in the absence of official definitions regarding what national parks and reserves actually are. By means of proposed bill deposited in 1937 the member of Parliament Robert Sérot tries to give a legal basis to the attempts to create parks and reserves but–once again, as in 1913–the outbreak of war interrupts the manoeuvre. Nevertheless, a unique personage, the surgeon and keen hunter Marcel Couturier from Grenoble, having become an eminent naturalist sponsors, from 1943, the creation of a national park like the Gran Paradiso to safeguard the ibex. After the war, he will be able to show his project to the international congress of administrators and directors of national parks organised in Cogne, in Val d'Aosta, on August 27, 1955 by the management of the Gran Paradiso National Park. During that year, your Consiglio Nazionale delle Ricerche expresses a vote supporting the project in the hopes of achieving a Franco-Italian park.

The 1960 law, as an accomplishment

The years following the war witness many other important people advocating and supporting the idea of national parks. In the wake of Georges Duhamel, writers, painters, and various artists rally round the new idea. Among them are the philosopher-farmer Gustave Thibon (1903-2001), the writer and historian Daniel-Rops (1901-1965), the novelist André Chamson (1900-1983), the writer, poet and water colourist Paul Gayet-Tancrède, universally known as Samivel (1907-1992), all bearers of a generous philosophy, humanistic but elitist, of national parks.

On the side of the scientists, many of those who had backed the creation of parks since before the war are still there. They take up the battle again and obtain from liberated France, in 1946, the establishment of a Conseil National de la Protection de la Nature with the duty of defining the statute of parks and reserves. In the following years the Council actively takes part in creating the Vanoise Park and in the formulation of the bill for parks, largely inspired by the preparatory work for the Vanoise.

In 1948 France is again at the forefront of a crucial event for the history of national parks, namely the founding at Fontainebleau of the Union Internationale pour la Protection, prepared by the Basel conference of 1946 and the Brunnen conference of 1947, both organised by the Ligue Suisse pour la Protection de la Nature in collaboration with UNESCO. It is a great success and a vote is again expressed for the creation of a national park in the forest of Fontainebleau. In 1956, during his mandate as president, Professor Roger Heim (1900-1979) will publish in the form of an annotated atlas of parks and reserves worldwide a book with a sensational and alarmist title: *Derniers refuges*.

We are nearing the conclusion. The law on national parks which will be voted in 1960 and the Vanoise National Park owe much to one man, Gilbert André (1927), from the Vosges, ensign in the battle against the degradation of mountains and mountain societies, a man who believes that mankind needs the mountains more than they need him. In 1952 he arrived in the village of Bonneval-sur-Arc to stay for a few weeks, but he will never leave it. From that moment André never stops work on "his" plan, the "creation of a cultural national park in the heart of the French Alps". An idealist, he defends the idea of an educational and regenerating park for the youth of the cities. On July 1, 1957 parliament votes an apparently marginal alteration to the registered sites in the 1930 law: the new article 8bis introduces the legal notion of natural reserves in place of sites classified as of scientific interest. It is from this moment, twenty years after Robert Sérot's proposal, that the path is re-opened toward the adoption of legislation regarding national parks.

November 6, 1957, in the presence of Gilbert André and fifteen or so politicians, administrators and authoritative intellectuals, the constitutive assembly of the Association des Parcs Naturels de France is held. During this meeting the general director of territorial management at the ministry of reconstruction and building explains in detail the plan for the creation of the future national park of the Vanoise to a young architect, Denys Pradelle (1913-1999):

> The park must consist of three concentric zones: 1. the outer zone, for human activity whose expansion must be encouraged; 2. from this first zone can be entered the second, smaller zone, without villages or cars, in which fauna and flora will be strictly safeguarded; 3. in the centre, finally, will be the zone for the integral protection of nature.

The V republic will begin soon after the decision to work on the law has been made. In 1959 the premier Michel Debré (1882-1978) asks the general director of Waters and Forests at the ministry of Agriculture, François Merveilleux du Vignaux (1902-1982), to "be quick". Vignaux gives the assignment to a young forestry engineer, Yves Bétolaud (1926-2003), responsible for a specialised nature protection cell in the ambit of the administration of Waters and Forests.

The text preparation is much influenced by the on-going debates concerning the Vanoise park project. The scientists are somewhat hostile to the idea of opening the park to the public, something that seems to them to contradict the idea of protection and hardly compatible with their research projects. Others on the contrary want to make the park widely open in order to offer compensation to the urban population deprived of contact with nature. Still others see a means of restoring big game populations or a means of development to help local populations in difficulty. Expectations are multiple and contradictory.

By adopting the radio centric scheme, Parliament establishes an apparent synthesis and creates the concept of "French-style" national parks with an *outer zone* making up a sort of "buffer zone", a *protected central zone* and within this a series of *integral reserves* forbidden to the general public and destined exclusively to scientific research. The land will be neither bought nor expropriated by the State, but will be made the object of a system of "bondage of public utility" inspired by the town-planning law and imposed on the owners. The law is promulgated on July 22, 1960; three years later, its application allows the founding of the first official French national park, the Vanoise.

New law, new national parks

The law of July 22, 1960 was quite a "light" one, made up of just eight articles. It founded–as Pierre Dumas will say forty years later– "revolutionary principles", and yet its application decree contained 46 articles capable of frightening even the most favourably disposed persons, such as Gilbert André, who complained: "if the law is relatively vague, the applied decree is extremely precise: it is a list of prohibitions! Everything is forbidden, except what is authorised by the director".

Not without difficulty, these founding texts allowed the creation of seven national parks. But at the end of the eighties the system folded because it was no longer keeping up with the evolution of society and the new management realities. An update was therefore necessary, and the new law of April 14, 2006 did just that. It strengthens the weight of park management collectivity and confirms its fundamental targets, but some innovations are introduced that are not only semantic:

- The *central zone* is now called the *heart of the park*. The power over fundamental decisions remains with the State for this zone, but the local communities have the right to be consulted;
- The *outer zone* is replaced by the *adherence area*, made up only of the municipalities which decide to be integrated in the park. To do this they sign a park *document* which is a territorial project lasting fifteen years aimed at conserving the heart of the park and its development;
- On the whole everything that now makes up the entity of national park, destined to put into perspective the notion of *ecological solidarity* among territories.

The reform has also allowed the creation of a coordinating organism of all the parks, called Parcs Nationaux de France. Following on from this legal evolution, in 2007 the passing of the creation of two new parks is concluded: the Amazonian park of Guyana and the Réunion . A third project is currently taking place–the earth and marine national park of Calanques, on the outskirts of Marseille. Another three parks are on-going, two forest ones including Fontainebleau and one in a wet zone. All these projects enter into the framework of the national strategy for creating protected areas set up by the law of August 3, 2009 relative to the establishment of the so-called *Grenelle de l'environnement*, the plan agreed on in 2007 between government and civil society with the aim of defining the main national political trends concerning ecology, development and long-term planning.

Bibliography

Fortier-Kriegel, Anne. 2010. La qualité des sites et des paysages en France ou l'histoire de la victoire des modernes. *Pour mémoire* 8: 88-99.

Gassot De Champigny, L. 1909. *La protection des sites et paysages*. Paris: Librairies des facultés A. Michalon.

Heim, Roger, Harroy, Jean- Paul, Caram, Marguerite and Jean-Jacques Petter. 1956. *Derniers refuges, Atlas commenté des Réserves Naturelles dans le monde*. Bruxelles: UICN-Elsevier.

Jaffeux, Henri. 2010. La longue et passionnante histoire des parcs nationaux français. *Pour mémoire* 9: 138-163.

Larrère Raphael, Lizet Bernadette and Martine Berlan-Darqué. 2009. *Histoire des parcs nationaux. Comment prendre soin de la nature?* Paris: Quæ.

Leynaud, Emile. 1985. *L'État et la nature: l'exemple des parcs nationaux français. Contribution à une histoire de la protection de la nature.* Florac: Ed. Parc national des Cévennes.

Martel, Edouard Alfred. 1913. La question des Parcs nationaux en France. *La Montagne. Revue du Club Alpin Français* IX : 402-408 and 433-457.

Mauz, Isabelle. 2003. *Histoire et mémoires du parc national de la Vanoise, 1921-1971: la construction.* Grenoble: Revue de géographie alpine" (collection "Ascendances").

—. 2005. *Histoire et mémoires du parc national de la Vanoise: trois générations racontent.* Grenoble: Revue de géographie alpine" (collection "Ascendances").

Mauz, Isabelle and Karine Larissa-Basset. 2010. Gilbert André. www.ahpne.fr/spip.php?article71

Merveilleux Du Vignaux, Pierre. 2003. *L'aventure des parcs nationaux. La création des parcs nationaux français, fragments d'histoire.* Montpellier: ATEN.

Sabatier, Michelle, Merveilleux Du Vignaux Pierre and Henri Jaffeux. 2010. *Pionniers. Aux origines des Parcs Nationaux: un album de famille*: Paris: Parcs Nationaux de France.

Selmi, Adel. 2006. *Administrer la nature. Le parc national de la Vanoise.* Paris: Editions de la Maison des sciences de l'homme.

VV.AA. 1937. *Contribution à l'étude des réserves naturelles et des parcs nationaux.* Paris: Société Française de Biogéographie.

—. 1957. *Réserves, parcs naturels de France. Rivières et Forêts* cahier n. 8.

—. 1971. *Les parcs nationaux, Compte-rendu du colloque international de Paris sur les parcs nationaux européens tenu à Paris, 15 au 17 juin 1970.* Paris: Fédération française des sociétés de sciences naturelles.

—. 1955. *Actes du premier congrès international des administrateurs et directeurs des parcs nationaux.* Turin: Ente Autonomo Parco Nazionale del Gran Paradiso.

SESSION III:

LONG TERM ASSESSMENTS

THE LOCAL COMMUNITIES IN THE HISTORY OF ABRUZZO NATIONAL PARK

ALBERTO D'ORAZIO

The relationship between local communities and the Park has ancient roots. In fact, it is possible to affirm that without the local communities and their political and institutional representatives the protected area would never have been born.

It is well-known in fact that the effective act marking the creation of the Park was the subscription between the Town of Opi and the Associazione Pro Montibus et Silvis of the lease contract of a small part of the Val Fondillo.

The idea of the Park had long taken root in the area thanks to some local personalities who had matured a view of the natural beauty, the biodiversity and the architectonical peculiarities of our towns as a harmonic whole to protect and, at the same time, exploit in a perspective of economic development of the territory. Today it is absolutely extraordinary to find in that far-sighted intuition, dating back to the beginning of the past century, the most topical concepts of conservation and sustainable development policies.

The constituent stage of the Abruzzo Park is marked, thus, by the presence of two fundamental elements: a view and project matured in well-rooted circles in the territory and the deliberative acts of the local governments that brought to fruition that view and that project.

Can we talk about a Park "born from below"? Even if with some caution, the answer can be affirmative, also because it is within a local and private initiative that the legislative models forming the basis of the establishment of the Park Authority as a public authority were elaborated. It was mainly thanks to this process "from the periphery to the centre" that the Authority was provided with autonomy and democratic management organs, in which local communities were widely represented.

However, it has to be remembered that the protagonists of the creation of the Park in 1922 represented an élite expression of the society of that time, characterized by deep cultural, social and wealth inequalities, so that the involvement of residents was not easy and their consensus was not sought with too much diligence. Nevertheless, the establishment of the Park undoubtedly represented a far-sighted effort for which today we have to thank all the protagonists, from the national scientific community to the local personalities, from the touristic associations to the mayors of the seven towns that were largely committed to the creation of the reserve.

Some later phenomena underlined the limits and contradictions of the initiative and reduced the expectations. Among them, it is necessary to remember the centralising force of fascism that led to the suppression of the Park Authority and the consequent bureaucratisation of its administration, the disaster of the war that imposed more concrete and immediate priorities than nature protection, the deep transformations of the national economy that caused a massive abandonment of the interior zones. All this while the Park was progressively reduced to a purely formal presence, without power or capacity of initiative, thus it was perceived by local communities exclusively as a source of bans and restrictions for both traditional and new economic activity. It was only from the 1960s, in concomitance with great political-social movements and the birth of environmentalist associations, that the matters concerning nature conservation and the cultural and economic role of the protected areas were topical again. This re-born interest, however, clashed with the growing rejection of the Park on the part of local communities, which considered the restrictions imposed by the conservation needs intolerable compared with the promises of the touristic economic development of those years.

The situation became even more difficult due to the evident contrast between, on the one hand, organisational difficulty and lack of planning ability of the Park Authority and, on the other hand, the success of business ventures in the construction field able to give immediate answers to the inescapable demand for work of residents who, with the demise of the agro-sylvan-pastoral economy, did not see an alternative to emigration. In such a situation it was not easy to defend the need to stop the speculative use of the territory and sustain a balanced growth of the residential and hotel property of the area without prejudicing the extraordinary natural and landscape value. It was then, however, that it became clear that this was the only true wealth able to give a stable and enduring economic perspective to the area.

This new view of development was embraced by a new generation of local administrators who, after achieving in the 1970s the leadership of the towns, was called to face the citizens' real problems: jobs, services, social cohesion, depopulation risks and the demand for a future on the part of the young generation. Cooperatives and associations were created and economic activities, based on the idea that "nature is development" were launched, and the Park began to be considered as a growth instrument for the local communities.

All these efforts required the instauration of constructive relations with all the institutional and economic subjects of the areas, including the Park Authority, which in those years was living a great period of re-launching and organisational renewal with the coming of the new director, Prof. Franco Tassi. A fruitful season began in which many young local people were involved and trained and who later would play important roles in the landscape of the Italian protected areas. The adoption of new and more advanced management models and the achievement of both a strong national and international visibility, allowed the Abruzzo National Park to become a strategic protagonist in Italian environmentalism. This undoubted success went together with a more and more pervasive local pivotal role that caused however numerous difficulties and disagreements.

It can be said that the local confrontation, that was already rather difficult, was complicated by the frequent attitudes of closure and, sometimes, of self-reference on the part of the Authority. There was much mutual incomprehension and, above all, many delays from the local communities in understanding the importance of the Park for the development of the area. Many local administrators, moreover, chose to set out their relations with the Park Authority on the basis of a more patronage than democratic view and this circumstance caused very serious damage to the credibility and the functioning of the Authority.

During the years, and also thanks to the issue of important norms on the representation of local communities in the administrative organs of protected areas, much of that incomprehension has been overcome. The Park has been able to widen its perimeter, which now includes a large portion of Molise territory, confirm its extension in the valleys of Lazio on the slopes of the historic peaks of the Petroso and Meta mounts and reach the Giovenco Valley up to the Fucino and, at the limit of the slopes of the Marsican, touch the spectacular Sagittario Valley.

By now it is an inter-regional Park, whose new denomination–since 2001 Abruzzo Lazio and Molise National Park–represents a great territorial, cultural and economic variety under the unifying sign of a natural heritage of extraordinary beauty.

The importance of the Park corresponds, on the other hand, to the importance of the Park Authority also on the employment front: in fact it directly employs more than one-hundred and ten workers–a labour force representing a huge resource for the territory–but indirectly occupies dozens of young people who, through small associations and without pre-constituted certainty, cooperate with passion as operators in the visitors' centres and in the faunal areas or as esteemed mountain guides.

Apart from all this, important difficulties remain and determine tension and resentment toward the Park that cannot be ignored. These difficulties are particularly evident in some delicate sectors: territorial and urban planning, choices concerning renewable energy, issues on livestock and the difficulties of farmers who have to be able to continue to play their precious role of protection of the territory, refunds for damage provoked by wild fauna, the internal organisation of the Authority, the way of using snow and, finally, the problem of confiding animals. For all these complex and delicate problems there is, however, the availability for confrontation and mutual comprehension that often lead to shared solutions. The majority of any remaining difficulties can be solved considering the Park Authority as the main reference for these problems and trying patiently to share all the choices in a democratic way.

On the other hand, in recent years there have been important changes in the protagonists' attitude: the Park Authority has shown a growing attention to the needs of towns and economic subjects while the local communities have acquired a stronger environmental sensibility that is linked to an ancient relationship of familiarity and respect toward nature and its resources. This relationship has been recently renewed and enriched when the local communities began to consider the territory as a fundamental part of their identity and the Park as the indispensable instrument for a growth that integrates nature conservation and economic planning.

Thus local communities today hold many expectations towards the Park, which has to play an ever more important role in the development of local economy which still remains uncertain, under many aspects. In fact it is characterised by the strong periodicity of tourism, the abandonment of the agricultural sector, serious difficulties for animal husbandry, very small firms, persistent difficulty to access credit and innovation, a high depopulation rate, the insufficiency of services and a low level of integration among the different economic sectors. The Park can give an important contribution to solving these problems, but it can do that only thanks to the cooperation of towns, provinces and the three regions whose territories lay in the protected area and to a common reflection on the best methods for making this collaboration more effective.

Besides this effort, it is necessary to think also about the role of the Park Community, the organ provided by the law of 1991 to allow the populations and institutions to participate actively in the management of the protected area. This very important role is often hindered by technical problems like the inadequate weight of the Community in the directive board of the Authority, the fact that the local election dates never coincide with the date of renewal of the organism's members and the delay in validating the appointments. These are apparently technical problems but they have a certain weight in the good functioning of the Community and, consequently, in the participation of the local residents in the life of the Park. To these local problems must be added the problems caused by a government policy that in recent years has not considered sustainable development and thus protected areas strategic and has been constantly influenced by the need to cut public spending to face crises. With this kind of policy, which ends with the curtailment of the incomes of the majority of the population, the fear is that there will be an uncertain and dark future especially for the local economies based on sectors like tourism.

What we have said up to now seems to prefigure some growing difficulties for the hypothesis that puts the Park at the centre of the working of the local economy. But we must not give up. The Abruzzo, Lazio and Molise National Park is today coming out of a long difficult period–well-illustrated by other speeches during this congress–that, however, has not undermined its national and international prestige and its capacity of attraction. There are still many things to do, some are difficult, but the local communities are determined to give their contribution and ask the government to adopt more efficient environmental policies, which can, at the same time, protect nature better and stimulate the economic development of peripheral areas like the upper Sangro.

The history of the Park has taught us that the efforts from above, although necessary, are not enough. The challenge for nature protection and the growth of our economy can be met only through the involvement and the active participation of local populations, who are interested in a development model based on the knowledge of environmental and territorial sources and the exaltation of their peculiarities. For a long time, the local communities of this area have invested their future on this model and, with the commitment to continue in this direction, proudly celebrate the ninetieth anniversary of the Abruzzo, Lazio and Molise National Park.

ENVIRONMENTAL LAW AND ETHICS: AUTONOMY OR UNION? THE ROLE OF PROTECTED NATURAL AREAS

GIANLUIGI CERUTI

Guido Fassò, in his *Storia della filosofia del diritto* (Fassò 2003, p. 200), authoritatively observed that "in the history of thought some reference to the distinction between juridical action and moral action is early and often found". And on this matter, expressions, in embryo, of such a distinction have been traced: in Ancient Greece in Democritus, Antiphon, Critias, Epicurus; in the Roman world, in the writings of the jurisconsult Paulo; by the end of the Middle Ages, in Marsilius from Padua; in the Renaissance, in Giordano Bruno and Paolo Paruta; among the Reformers, in the Swiss Ulrich Zwingli.

But it was the German philosopher and jurist Christian Thomasius (1655-1728) who in the work *Fundamenta juris naturae et gentium* (Halle 1718) theorised the distinction between *justum* and other two forms of human action, *honestum* and *decorum*, and *honestum* is synonymous of *moral*.

Felice Battaglia in his monograph *Cristiano Thomasio filosofo e giurista* (Battaglia 1936, p. 222) clearly explained the elements of Law as it is defined by the German thinker:

Right is the norm regulating the actions of two subjects: a subject can claim a behaviour to which another is obliged. The opposite of right and obligation is wrong or negated right. Whence it results that for Thomasius right is not admissible if not in the sort of intersubjectivity, so that exteriority, where no one has a right on himself, no one can oblige himself to himself or do wrong to himself: "Patet igitur, quod jus, item obligatio externa juri correspondens, et injuria, semper supponant duos homines. Unde nemo habet proprie jus in se ipsum, nec sibi injuriam facere potest, nec sibi obligatur" (Fundamenta juris naturae et gentium, 1. I c. V). It is therefore evident how right, equal to obligation which is the external correspondent of right, and also its violation, always implies two men. Consequently, no one can really have a right toward himself or can do wrong to himself or can oblige himself: "Jus omne externum est, non internum. Ergo eadem dicenda sunt de obligatione jure respondente, i.e. externa" (Fundamenta juris naturae et gentium, 1. I c. V, "Every right is external, not internal. Consequently the same thing can be said about obligation that corresponds to right, namely that it too is external").

Thomasius affirms that Law disciplines the relations among two or more men and can pretend from the one obliged the observance of his right through forcibility, thus with the possible resort to coercion, while moral poses the duties of man toward himself, thus working in the internal sphere.

The distinction between moral and right will find a more complete formulation in Immanuel Kant's works *Grundlegung Zur Metaphysik der Sitten* (1785) and *Metaphysik der Sitten* (1797).

After Kant the distinction of the juridical sphere from the ethical one has been constantly reaffirmed and the logical elements of the Law characterising the juridical action with respect to the moral one have been outlined as intersubjectivity, exteriority and forcibility.

Now, it is difficult not to agree with the above mentioned definitions. However, even being aware that in humanity's history and in the events concerning spirit and thought it is arbitrary to determine the date of the start of a movement, we can approximately place in the nineteenth century the first important expressions of the need to fix a defensive shield, with normative instruments and juridical remedies, against negative, even serious, implications for the psychophysical integrity of man and the healthiness of air that appeared with the advance of the industrial revolution.

So the pollution produced by the use of coal in the industrial factories and the fuelling of trains is at the origin of the reactions of two English authors, John Ruskin and William Morris, who in 1863 advocated the need for health protection.

Backed by public opinion movements–worried by the damage to life and landscape beauty that could be caused by uncontrolled industrialisation or the excessive exploitation of natural resources–there were legislative measures in England, Bavaria, in the Grand Duchy of Hesse, in Prussia, Austria, Belgium and in the Helvetic Confederation. In France at the beginning of the nineteenth century the painter Henri Regnault, one of the promoters of the association called Ligue pour la Conservation de Sites Pictoresques founded to preserve the Fontainebleau forest, launched a message: "The forest is loved by the artist and the dreamer because it is beautiful, but should be more beloved by every utilitarian spirit because it is indispensable for man, for his health and survival".

In the second half of the twentieth century, in the most industrialised countries, begins a season that is destined to last as long as activities detrimental to human wellbeing, forms of animal and vegetal life, the integrity of landscape in its morphological and cultural aspects, the environment (a concept which starts to take shape in these years) with the alteration of the elements essential to the survival of the ecosystems and threats of extinction of faunal and floristic species and life on earth itself continue to exist.

At the beginning of the second half of the last century, the great American ecologist Aldo Leopold powerfully summarised the essence of the ethical duties of human beings toward other living beings and the universe, in a moment when all over the world the deep wounds, inferred by a recent collective tragedy where man had violated, overturned and destroyed fundamental and essential coexistence values, equilibriums, ecosystems and nature landscapes, works built by effort and intelligence, were healing: the recent atomic explosions of Hiroshima and Nagasaki and their consequences are an example. Leopold said:

> A land ethic changes the role of *Homo sapiens* from conqueror of the land-community to plain member and citizen of it. It implies respect for his fellow-members, and also respect for the community as such. [...] Examine each question in terms of what is ethically and aesthetically right, as well as what is economically expedient. A thing is right when it tends to preserve the integrity, stability, and beauty of the biotic community. It is wrong when it tends otherwise. (Leopold 1949)

The range of unhealthy activities that generate multiple–even serious and sometimes lethal–forms of pollution (radioactive, atmospheric, hydric and acoustic) contaminating sometimes also the ground and aquifers is vast: some examples are variously supplied power plants, rubbish incineration, disposal and processing plants, extraction, working and production of some carcinogenic types of asbestos, emission of fine dusts, polycyclic aromatic hydrocarbon, carbon and sulphur dioxide, dioxin and furan, quarries, tanneries, breeding farms and road infrastructures.

To avoid or, at least, limit and reduce the serious hygienic-sanitary damage, individuals and committees of residents of the threatened and attacked zones have opposed and still oppose and, in the name of high ethical ideals and with spirit of solidarity, sacrifice time and money to safeguard the living conditions of their communities. They have to oppose public institutions that frequently do not pursue the general interest, even if this should be their task, but, often pushed by conspicuous private and personal interests together with forms of corruption, approve or validate with their decisions the realization of works that often undermine the fundamental ethical value of life and, in some cases, are sources of collective massacres, as proved by the facts that occurred in Bhopal, Seveso, Marghera, Chernobil, Casale Monferrato, Fukushima, just to mention some of the most lacerating and tragic events of the last fifty years, ascribable to the criminality and irresponsibility of man, his avidity for money, his greed for power and, sometimes, even if to a lesser extent, his ignorance.

The topic of protected natural areas represents a fascinating open book that every year is enriched with new pages and, according to the famous definition of the President of the United States Franklin Delano Roosevelt, measures the civilization of a people.

With the establishment of parks and nature reserves, limited portions of the planet are destined to have a rational and non-destructive use of natural resources for the spiritual and physical wellbeing of everyone.

After the American experiences of the Hot Springs natural reserves in Arkansas (1832) for the protection of petrified forests, the Sierra Nevada valleys (1864) and the Yellowstone (1872) and Yosemite (1890) national parks, the nature conservation through protected areas had a thriving explosion in the other continents. In 1879 Australia founded its first national park, today called Royal National Park. On June, 23 1887 the Federal Government of Canada, under the direct and personal impulse of its premier John Mac Donald, established the Banff National Park. In the same year, New Zealand created the Tongoriro National Park. In 1898 in South Africa was founded the Sabie Natural Reserve to which was added in 1903 that of Singwitsi (or Singwedsi); later (1926) these two reserves will represent the original core of the Kruger National Park. In 1909 in Sweden were created nine national parks: Abisko, Stona Sjöfallet, Janek, Pielgekaise, Sonfjallet, Hamma, Ganphyttaw, Angso and, in part, Gotska Sandon. The first national park of Central Europe was the Swiss park of Engadine (1914). In 1919 in Poland the forest of Białowieża was reserved to total protection. In 1921, due to the initiative of the Federazione nazionale Pro Montibus et Silvis, the Park Authority of the Abruzzo National Park was established and in December of 1922 there was the measure that ratified the creation of the Gran Paradiso National Park. And the initiatives for new protected areas continued and still continue all over the world.

The common feature is the conservation of valuable and endangered natural resources, inherited from past generations to be safeguarded, to be preserved and handed down "for the benefit and enjoyment of future generations".

This call to the care and responsibility of present generations recurs often in the normative documents concerning the maintenance of natural resources especially in the field of protected natural areas and it has a high ethical significance that echoes the passage of the Bible of the Genesis about the role and the commitment of man in using and preserving for the future the heritage entrusted by his forefathers.

Revising the formation paths and the founding acts of the first protected natural areas it is possible to reap the substantial reason that is the cultural basis at the root of the decision to create this or that park, this or that natural reserve. Yellowstone National Park is not born suddenly, but is the result of a process of gradual cultural and political ripening nourished by a public opinion movement that rose in the first half of the eighteenth century and influenced by the poet and painter George Catlin that had a wide circulation in the United States.

The mobilisation of wide sectors of the North-American population grew in the second half of the century around an eminent judge, Cornelius Hedges, who appealed to Congress and presented a proposal for the creation of Yellowstone National Park:

> God made this region for all the people and all the world to see and enjoy forever. It is impossible that any individual should think that he could own any of this country for his own and in fee. This great wilderness does not belong to us, but to America. Let us make a public park of it and set it aside for America, never to be changed, but kept sacred just as it is now, so that Americans always may know how splendid this early America was, how beautiful, how wonderful.

The President of the United States Ulysses Grant signing the Act with which on March, 1 1872 Yellowstone became a national park (the first in the world) commented the historical event declaring that no other measure was followed (in his own words) by such

> Great approval inside and so much profusion of congratulations from abroad, marking an innovation in the traditional policy of the Government: from time immemorial privileged classes have been protected by law in the withdrawal, for their exclusive enjoyment, of immense tracts for forests, parks and game preserves. But never before was a region of such vast extent as the Yellowstone Park set apart for the use of all the people without distinction of rank or wealth.

Since 1962 the International Union for the Conservation of Nature (today World's Conservation Union, UICN according to the original French acronym and IUCN, to the English one) has promoted, every ten years, the World Parks Equivalent Reserves Congress, where the great subjects (philosophical, scientific, political and economic themes) concerning the survival of human society, the conservation of biological diversities are debated together with the main problems related to the working of the different categories of protected natural areas of the Planet.

The Congresses–held until now in the Grand Teton, in Seattle, Bali, Caracas and Durban–end with a final document that is a sort of lay catechism of conservation, a *summa* of universally accepted principles and orientations. The final declaration of the First Congress (Seattle 1962) affirmed that the beauty and character of landscapes and sites are necessary for human life, have a great spiritually regenerating influence, from the physical and moral point of view and contribute to the artistic and cultural life of peoples.

According to the world congress of Bali (1982)

National parks' and other protected areas' contribution to the people and life on earth is fundamental for the search for wellbeing, the quality of life and an enduring peace; with the vision of an equally ambitious and vital challenge just as every challenge in human history; and with a commitment of solidarity toward our sons and future generations with the purpose of inheriting this unique, small and fragile planet.

Environmental Law, which preserves the logical elements identified by the philosophical-juridical tradition in that it is provided with bilaterality (or intersubjectivity), exteriority and forcibility, innovatively introduces a characteristic of diversity and this is the main assumption, the thesis proposed here: the Environmental Law is not autonomous from Ethics, but it is linked to it by an indissoluble tie, a permanent bond, a tight alliance: it is innate.

From its first experiences and expressions in human history the Environmental Law originates from mainly ethical needs and has moral contents and aims with the objective–having priority over any other interest–to defend and preserve life, persons and other living being, the equilibrium of ecosystems from any and every hidden danger and injury.

The consequences of this idea on public administration action and jurisdictional experiences are not small matters. In fact, every time it has to be assessed in administrative sittings if an activity, a work, a potentially harmful action (in industry, agriculture or infrastructures) can be authorised or in the judicial ambit it has to be decided if the relative administrative acts are legitimate, the so-called "balance of interests" cannot have any justification once scientifically proved elements are evaluated which consider that that activity, that work, that intervention are potentially harmful to primary values like health, life, the environment and ecosystems' integrity, they are not comparable with the economic and political interests for the realisation; and the certainty of the damage cannot be pretended because the reasonable perspective that such realisation might cause harm to the general interest suffices.

The principles of preventive and precautionary action, regulated by the current Treaty of the European Union, should always be present in the public administrators' and judges' decision: in case of doubt, the option should be in favour of the land-ethic, the protection of the fundamental values of health, safety, intangibility of life, the survival of coexistence conditions, the cultural identity of a community.

Bibliography

Battaglia, Felice. 1936. *Cristiano Thomasio filosofo e giurista*. Rome: Società Editrice del Foro Italiano.

Fassò, Guido. 2003. *Storia della filosofia del diritto. L'età moderna*, updated by Carla Faralli. Bari-Rome: Laterza.

Leopold, Aldo. 1949. *A Sand County Almanac*. New York: Oxford University Press.

The Abruzzo National Park and the Evolution of the Protected Area Concept in Italy

Carlo Alberto Graziani

1. The subject that I intend to deal with concerns the role played by the Abruzzo National Park in the evolution of the concept of park and, in general, of protected areas in Italy and maybe outside Italy. It is a theme that perhaps requires the objectivity of a scholar, in particular of a historian and jurist.

But I am not a historian so I hope that what I say will pass critical examination, especially by Luigi Piccioni, the Italian historian of parks who, together with the President of the Park, is to be credited with the organisation of this conference. I am a jurist, but today I do not mean to play this role because I want to be a witness whose roots lie deep in this land, in the upper Sangro.

I am conscious of the limits of my evidence–the partial and biased view, the lack of objectivity–but I am also convinced of its merit, because it shows subjective motivations and dynamics which surely help understand and reconstruct events.

I have had the chance to follow–in the sense of living them critically– the events of the Abruzzo National Park (ANP) for almost half a century. It has been an experience that has deeply marked and directed my life and my professional and political activity. In the light of this experience I will try to let the facts talk.

2. The late 1960s mark a fundamental turn in the history of the Abruzzo National Park. The town of Pescasseroli is the most important centre of local tourism and houses the offices of the Park; its territory has been victim to touristic speculation for more than a decade. Unscrupulous landowners and builders, with the connivance of local administrators, have given life to a widespread property operation which has deeply modified the landscape and with it, traditions, ways of life as well as rights. Yes, rights, because nearly every building is erected on lands encumbered by collective use, that is, old rights belonging to the population (especially the right to graze cattle) which the town council should have protected.

Precisely in these years, however, the events of the Park intersect the spreading of a new sensitivity towards environmental issues. Thanks to the work of journalists of great quality, especially of Antonio Cederna from the *Corriere della Sera*'s columns, to the initiatives of the main environmentalist associations, particularly Italia Nostra, the Club Alpino Italiano and the WWF (the Italian appeal launched by Fulco Pratesi and others dates back to 1966), and, from 1969, to the important role played by the new director, Franco Tassi, coming from the ranks of the WWF, the Park becomes a focus of attention all over Italy as well as abroad.

Of course, at the local level it is easy for speculators to affirm that tourist and ski resorts represent the historical occasion to finally take the road of development after centuries of suffering and migration related to a pastoral economy in crisis. It is also very easy to accuse journalists and environmentalists, as well as the new Directorate, of wanting to expel the population from its own territory for the enjoyment of the "people from the city".

The atmosphere gets heated and the relations between populations and the Park bear the brunt of it, and its consequences will weigh heavily in the following years. The conflict shows complexity and contradictions.

There is the pride of the representatives of local populations, aware that the Park is the result of their participation: that participation displayed from the beginning when in 1921, thanks to the passionate work of an extraordinary personality from Pescasseroli, the MP Erminio Sipari, the towns of Pescasseroli, Opi, Civitella Alfedena, Gioia and Lecce de' Marsi, Villavallelonga and Bisegna assigned the most beautiful and naturalistically rich of their areas to the Park in the making. There is the idea of the importance of touristic development, but at the same time the contrast among different views of tourism and development. There is mainly the clash, which is not a contradiction, between a strongly local culture (however it is not always internally homogeneous) and a new rising culture, the environmentalist one.

The future of the upper Sangro and with it the Abruzzo mountain and the entire Apennine is in the running and it is a game played between the perspective of a touristic development that is tearing nature and consciences, risking to tear them even more, and the hope and will to preserve that nature.

3. The perspective of touristic development was old and coeval to the establishment of the Park. I underline this especially important aspect: I do this following the thought of its founder. According to Erminio Sipari the

Park was an occasion to introduce a new economy able to redeem the populations: "touristic industrialisation"–as he called the new economy–, interrupting a centuries-old isolation, would bring the elevation of their civilised and economic standard of life. For many years, with obstinacy, he proposed his belief.

But–he wondered, anticipating possible criticism–does not this "industrialisation" carried out inside a Park contradict the American view of parks from which we draw inspiration? Those cultural élites who in Italy struggled to defend "natural beauty" considered by Luigi Piccioni the first Italian movement for nature protection–of whom Sipari was an expression–were inspired by the view established in the United States at the end of the nineteenth century. And effectively a tourist-oriented park seemed to distance itself from that model which was spreading in Europe as well–apart from the then unknown parks established by Sweden in Lapland in 1909, and the Swiss National Park created in 1914 in Engadine–and risked being in contradiction with the contemporary Gran Paradiso Park.

In the accurately documented report presented on May 17, 1923, day of assignment of the administrative board of the ANP Authority, the Park president replied:

> The best is enemy of the good, the preoccupation with always wanting to solve every problem in a perfect way on paper paralyses and prevents action; if we had stopped our work of pushing in favour of the establishment of the Park, to delve into theoretical distinction or to wait for the different Italian minds to agree on the form to give to Italian national parks, we would have seen the bears destroyed by the relentless research being done in the last two years by museums, naturalists and amateurs. On the other hand, it is utopian to believe that Italy can ever achieve the miracle of finding a single type of park for its diverse regions.

A sane realism, thus, joined to the clarity of objectives and a great tenacity in pursuing them shows us the success of Erminio Sipari's action. Outcome of this perseverance was the inclusion of "touristic and hotel industry development" among the purposes of the founding law of January 1923, together with the fauna, flora, geological formations and landscape conservation which the legislator attributed to the Gran Paradiso National Park when, just a month earlier, it had been established.

It has to be incidentally noted that the foundation of the Abruzzo Park in 1921, to which I referred earlier, was the result of private (but not less important) enterprise of the Federazione Pro Montibus–a very active association in those years–which, thanks to Sipari's work, after leasing the lands from the towns, had created the "Authority of the Abruzzo National Park", a denomination taken over by law.

In Erminio Sipari's thought the park was not a mere instrument for touristic development; his idea was not the anticipation of that banal ideology supported today by the horrible word "anthropisation": it contained, instead, the fertile intuition of the conciliation among different but not contrasting goals. On the basis of this intuition he accomplished his work.

In the monograph of Pescasseroli, published by Benedetto Croce in the appendix of his *Storia del Regno di Napoli*, there is a trace of the role played by his cousin, the founder of the Park:

> And another thought was dreamt of, and its supporter was the engineer Sipari: that this green valley at one thousand two hundred meters, surrounded by mountains and hills, with woods centuries-old or resurgent due to new reforestation, just a few hours distant from Rome, might become a health resort and hotels might be erected.

Some years ago it was possible to read this passage on the façade of the big hotel built at the beginning of the 1960s representing one of the first scandals, maybe at that time the most clamorous. The specious use of the words of the philosopher of Pescasseroli represented one episode in the struggle engaged by property speculation against the Park Authority. Today those words no longer appear on that wall, evidence of a new cultural atmosphere, of a more respectful coexistence.

The integration of tourism among the goals of Abruzzo National Park marked a qualitative passage of great, although not always felt, relevance in the philosophy and history of protected areas. Since then the concept of park (and also, at least in Italy, of national park) is not linked to the original idea of "wilderness" areas–like the big American parks and the first European parks among them, substantially, the Gran Paradiso– intended for spiritual enjoyment and consequently for scientific research that guarantees the conservation of natural resources and therefore of that enjoyment. With the founding law of the Abruzzo National Park the legislator chose to determine the conciliating principle of conservation and development purposes: an irreversible choice around which the history of these ninety years has revolved .

It is a complex history made up of conflicts as well as contradictions. The contradictions can be summarised in two images, both of ruins: modern, not ancient ruins. The first is that of the ruins erected in the middle of the Camosciara plain, result of the idea of a big hotel advocated by Erminio Sipari since 1909. This idea had led in the 1950s to a senseless choice of the Park Authority itself: the destruction of the Medieval Rocca tra' monti in order to build a hotel in that same place. The unfinished work is a strict warning: those who fight for a good cause can also be wrong, even if they love nature.

The other image, in remarkable contrast to the first, is that of the ruins of the Cicerana, result of the very harsh struggle victoriously fought by the Park Authority in the 1970s and 1980s against speculation thanks to the brave and tenacious action led by Franco Tassi (however, as we will see, not only by him). Those ruins too, even if of an opposite significance because they are not the result of love but of contempt for nature, remain as an everlasting reminder of human folly.

4. The years between the 1960s and the 1970s are also the years of student protests. The protest could not avoid involving this territory too.

On December 12, 1970 in Milano Saverio Saltarelli, 23 years-old, from Pescasseroli, is killed by a tear gas bomb fired at eye level during a demonstration for the first anniversary of the Piazza Fontana bombing. One year later Pescasseroli is invaded by a multitude of students who want to remember their comrade. In the square, on the balcony of the town hall, waves, for the first time, a red flag that predicts change.

Pescasseroli watches astonished, but not hostile. Saverio was one of its sons: in winter he studied in Milan (first at the high school then at the university), in summer he returned to the town; to pay for his studies, he had occasional jobs both in Milan and Pescasseroli. The previous summer he had organised a group of student workers from the residence construction site to denounce the overexploitation of the seasonal workers forced to work up to 14 hours per day without national insurance: he was immediately fired, but he did not stop struggling against uncontrolled speculation, and the devastation of the Park and denouncing the mayor's connivance.

The revolt inflaming the Italian universities where other young people from the towns of the Park studied–mainly in Rome–has already infected this territory too: the Movimento popolare Alta Valle del Sangro (Upper Sangro Valley Popular Movement) is born and carries on Saverio's struggle. It is not just a fight against power, represented by the Christian Democracy which for more than twenty-five years has dominated uncontested the whole area thanks to its political patronage, and a part of which has built up a perverse alliance with the construction speculation; it is also a fight for the salvation of the territory and therefore of the Park. The relationship with the earth, which represents an important vein, even if subterranean, of the student movement culture mainly among the non-resident students from the South, gives specific weight to the struggle fought by the Upper Sangro young people and opens up a new vision of the parks.

We are anchored to a reconstruction that puts the evolution of the idea of park in Italy on a path which starts at the beginning of the twentieth century with the movement I mentioned above, continues with the establishment of the Abruzzo and Gran Paradiso national parks, stops during fascism and the war, starts again in the 1960s thanks to the Commission for research into nature conservation of the Centro Nazionale delle Ricerche animated by Alessandro Ghigi, to Italia Nostra, the WWF and personalities such as Renzo Videsott, whose importance today appears in all its significance thanks to Franco Pedrotti's and Luigi Piccioni's works, becomes incandescent in the 1970s and 1980s around the facts of the Abruzzo National Park brought to the general attention by the important press, involves scholars such as Valerio Giacomini, but at the same time lingers in a wearying extra-parliamentary and then parliamentary debate on the framework law–to which the new experience of the regional parks brings not only new nourishment but also moments of paralysing controversies–, to come to an end, finally, thanks to the commitment of the Greens for the first time in Parliament, with the issuing of the Law no. 394/1991, the framework law.

This reconstruction, however, does not explain why and how an idea of park, different from the original, which does not put at the margins or even ban the issue of development and human presence, making it instead a fundamental matter, established itself; it does not do justice to the explosive, although not without ingenuity, action led here in the towns of the Park by the young people who from 1974 to 1980 succeed in changing the political aspect of the Upper Sangro and obtain this result without waving the easy anti-park flag, as until then town administrators and local politicians had done, but fighting against construction speculation for a vision of the park able to combine conservation and development and to make populations full protagonists of the territory's management.

The action of those young people in Abruzzo becomes unanimous because it involves an important part of the trade union and politics. The most influential trade union, the CGIL, lines up, in absolutely original ways for the Italian union view, an intransigent defence of the territory and embraces the new idea of park emerging from the Upper Sangro. At the same time the seed sown by those young people within their party of reference, the PCI, contributes to overtake the industrial and "development" (as it is called today) logic of that party and to reconsider some theoretical consolidated positions on the parks issue. The consideration involving the Abruzzo PCI meets on a central level the sensitivity of two important personalities such as Raffaello Misiti and Giovanni Berlinguer: the Grosseto conference of 1984 wanted by them will be the signal of a deep change which was maturing within the PCI and which in the following years would be fundamental to approve the framework law. But the young people's action will also be useful to reshape the influence of the plunderer mayor of the Cicerana, Mario Spallone, Togliatti's doctor, who the PCI will not candidate to the Senate.

These, often ignored, facts are in my opinion important to reconstruct the evolution not only in Abruzzo of the idea of park and thus they have to be considered by those who want to write the Italian history of the parks.

5. The new view of the park is not in conflict with the dominant one, but inserts elements of fertile diversity. Even if it is watched with scepticism and from a distance by the park Authority and the many others– well-known associations and journalists–who support its action, it inevitably ends, however, in "contaminating" the traditional view.

We are in the 1970s: in the other important national park managed by an Authority, the Gran Paradiso, the importance of the traditional idea of park is confirmed, thanks mainly to the great contribution offered in the previous decades by Renzo Videsott. Here too the speculation attack is strong, but the relationship between conservation and development does not emerge in all its complexity because it is a sparsely populated territory. For the same reason it does not emerge in the national parks managed by the Corpo Forestale dello Stato (State Forestry Corps). On the other hand, the regional parks, which in general are made up of , sometimes intensely-populated areas (an example is the Lombard Ticino Park, the first regional park established in 1975), in those years timidly begin to appear in the national context and are not yet able to influence the debate. If we, then, look closer to us, at the experience of the French regional parks–the most similar to the peculiarities of our, also national, parks–it is still at the beginnings and, above all, is little known in Italy.

It is precisely here, in this territory, that the problem of the relationship between conservation and development explodes; it is around this park that conflicts, controversies, harsh debates focus; it is here that slowly the idea of compatibility matures, an idea that, half a century before and in an easier situation Erminio Sipari had intuited; it is here that the idea of park as laboratory of experimentation of a different way of managing the territory appears, a place where it is possible to reach high-level compromise between rigorous conservation and effective compatible development.

Maybe the fear that high-level compromises cannot exist, that any compromise has to be necessarily at a low level, leads the Park Authority and its supporters to look with suspicion at the idea of a different viewpoint

I remember the conversations and the correspondence with Antonio Cederna, the fruitless effort to convince him that the local framework was changing, that supporting the new ideas was important, that the emerging strengths represented a great opportunity fot the Park and not a mere instrument at the Authority's disposal. I remember similar meetings with Franco Tassi. But I clashed against a wall made up of incomprehension and diffidence.

The miracle of Civitella Alfedena–which the freelance press has considered for years an extraordinary result of the new management of the Park–has to be interpreted thinking about this wall and at the same time in the light of an instrumental use which did not appear on the outside.

That miracle was possible not only–in contrast to what the press wrote–for the will of the Park Authority, but also mainly thanks to the far-sighted action of some young people, led by the mayor (Giuseppe Rossi, today president of the Park), who operated with the clear aim of giving economic and cultural strength to their town, creating a new touristic business for the territory integrated with the Park and in harmony with the Authority.

It was one of the dreams, there would be many, and at that time perhaps one of the most interesting, of a deep change which was involving the towns of the Park, expression of a more general phenomenon concerning the whole Italian society. That change, if the importance had been understood, would have represented the chance of an extraordinary alliance between the hegemonic institution, the Park Authority, and the young component of local society.

6. The new culture needs participation. If we wanted to introduce a schematic and simplified periodization, we could say that the 1980s for the Park territory are the years focused on the participation issue. This participation is the result of a change caused by the local election outcome of 1974 in Pescasseroli and of 1975 in Civitella Alfedena and Opi, which in the 1980 election spreads to the whole Upper Sangro: this territory traditionally dominated by the Christian Democracy opens almost completely to the left thanks to the aggregating action of the young members of the Movimento popolare Alta Valle del Sangro which finds in the PCI the political point of reference and, as I have already mentioned, contributes to give an environmentalist conscience to this party on a regional, but not exclusively, level.

The change is not just political, but mainly cultural and is rooted in the new vision of the park.

The main point for any town administrator is the management of the territory: thus, for the new administrators of the Upper Sangro's towns the participation in the management of the Park is pivotal. In that period there is no law fixing specific norms; of course, there are the general principles starting from the constitutional ones, but the interpretation is very complex and could be interesting for the theoretical jurist. It is more important, also because it is urgent, to create concrete relations, face problems directly, open new perspectives. The Park—meant as institution and territory— becomes a real workshop of ideas and experiments, but also inevitably of new conflicts. Up for discussion there is no longer as the main issue (it is only partially important) the construction land-use of the areas; there is instead the issue, demanded by the new administrators, of their effective participation in the management of the territory to achieve the electoral programs on which bases they have been elected and which are, at least generally, coherent with the existence of the Park.

The director, Franco Tassi, launches the proposal of a Park Community; a place to discuss the choices of the Park Authority with the town representatives. The Community, initially welcomed, is a failure: the administrators do not just want to be heard, they want to participate in the decision making.

The Park Authority goes along its way. The director seems always stronger: he leads the Park onto the national and international scene; he wins the many court battles into which he is forced or which he obstinately engages; the important press stays with him and the "10% Challenge" launched by him in 1980 from Camerino has a great echo; construction speculation is de facto defeated, indubitably thanks to his action, made possible, as I have already said, by the context that is the action of the young people of the Upper Sangro (so, for example, the writings "Down with Tassi" at night time become "Down with Grassi", the most important constructor of Pescasseroli) and by the clear change of the Abruzzo political framework and the peculiarities of the local administrations: however, all this does not emerge on the outside; on the other hand, the old politics that have long worked by various, more or less subterraneous means to remove Franco Tassi do not obtain any result. From this position of force, the director does not intend to link the action of the Park to the effective involvement of the administrators, who—he thinks—remain expressive of that politics or, at least, are influenced by it. He does not consider that the new administrators not only have their own autonomy, but are also bearers of that new culture which could represent an extraordinary strength for the Park. In this way, an opportunity that will never be repeated is lost.

It is a huge limit and it will weigh heavily on the management of the Park, marking the start of the Authority's isolation and it will be one of the causes of a deep institutional crisis.

But that idea of a Park Community remains because it is fertile; it improves itself evolving in the direction hoped for by the new town administrators: the framework law will accept the model and confer a relevant decisional role to the Park Community.

The history of the Abruzzo National Park contributes to point out the solution for the administrative board as well. Its composition in the name of the pluralism which will be conferred by the framework law is linked to the model provided by the instituting laws of 1922-23, but, above all, is the result of debates, practices, experiments which have characterised the Abruzzo National Park's life and have shown the possibility of a synthesis between local and general needs and at the same time the potentiality of the relationship between such needs.

7. From the 1970s, thanks also to Civitella Alfedena's example, a phenomenon that soon spreads in the Park and then in all Italian protected areas is outlined: young women and men gather in groups, become members of cooperatives to manage services useful to the protected area especially in the touristic sector (campsites, hostels, guide service, management of museums, park houses and information centres), but also in the agricultural sector.

It is a huge, original phenomenon born from the wish to remain anchored to their land, the will to build here their path of life and work, the need for simple values like nature, but great like its protection, in other words from the new culture of the park. This phenomenon, that is not a commercial expression but an ideal ambition, is at the service of the protected areas cause, of their mission. The economical reward obtained by those young women and men with their working activities is greatly inferior to the value of the offered services of which the institution avails itself: generosity is priceless.

Not just in the Abruzzo National Park but in all Italian protected areas those young women and men represent a potentially huge force. If only the institutions would notice it, if the people in charge would let the phenomenon emerge and organise it.

But another wall of diffidence is erected in front of this innovation, a phenomenon that to exist and develop needs autonomy and rejects instrumental use. Yet again I want to be a witness, but I am a sad witness. How many meetings to push the Park Authority to support the cooperatives in their autonomy, to trust them! How many meetings with the Lega delle Cooperative to illustrate the potentiality of the phenomenon, the need to organise it! How many meetings with the Lega per l'ambiente (at that time this was the name of Legambiente) so that it would get involved in supporting the cooperatives in the parks!

The wall of diffidence was–and sadly still is–insurmountable. In short, these are the replies: cooperatives are politicised and linked to local logics, so it is impossible to fully trust them, we can only use them; parks' cooperatives are weak economic subjects so it is not worth taking action to organise them; cooperatives cannot be labelled by us because they are linked to the parks' management authorities, on the contrary, it is better if the link with the institutions is broken otherwise it becomes welfare.

Yet, despite criticism and obstacles, in spite of the extreme economic weakness and the proud claims of autonomy, the phenomenon of the groups remains a peculiarity of the protected areas territory. Thanks also, and maybe mainly, to ever more qualified actions accomplished by these groups, new professions giving strength and substance to protected areas are established.

In this case as well the example of the Abruzzo National Park contributes in a determinative way to show a path which, even if it is not accepted in the framework law, will characterise what we can call the material establishment of protected areas.

8. Conclusion. The Abruzzo National Park–meant in its complexity: institution and territory; administrators and civil society, rather community–has played a general role for many years. Its mission has been to affirm the park culture in Italy, a non-ideological culture, not closed in on itself but open to the evolution of the times, to the contributions of the people who have worked for the park, within or outside it: for love, more than for institutional duty, for work, or for political vocation.

The historical mission of the Abruzzo National Park, its role in general, was accomplished in 1991 after the framework law and the explosion of new national and regional parks. It is fair that it was like this, because since then the mission has been entrusted to all protected areas, not to just one of them. I would like to be able to say that the mission is entrusted to the system of protected areas: sadly, we cannot yet say that for various reasons impossible even to list here.

For this common mission every park–the Abruzzo National Park too (today Abruzzo, Lazio and Molise National Park)–has to give its own contribution which will be more precious the more the park learns from its history, best uses its resources, succeeds in availing itself of the many people who work or would like to work for its success.

In a period in which everything becomes market, in a society where everything can be exchanged for money, where financial logics impose their choices, the fundamental challenge is to rediscover the ideal value of parks which is linked to the care of the earth: an intense care, in the fullest meaning of the word. Parks in fact represent models for a territorial management marked by a fundamental principle that should lead political initiative and the action of every single person: the earth belongs to everyone, it is our destiny, we are all responsible for it.

Bibliography

Arnone Sipari, Lorenzo (ed.). 2011. *Scritti scelti di Erminio Sipari sul Parco nazionale d'Abruzzo (1922-1933).* Temi: Trento.

Cederna, Antonio. 1975. *La distruzione della natura in Italia.* Turin: Einaudi.

Croce, Benedetto. 1925. *Storia del Regno di Napoli.* Bari: Laterza.

De Lucia, Vezio and Giuseppe Cederna. 2006. Il bell'Antonio. *Parchi* 48: 83 et seq.

Giacomini, Valerio. 1977. Evoluzione e attualità del concetto di Parco Nazionale. *La ricerca scientifica. Rendiconti dell'attività del Consiglio Nazionale delle Ricerche* (Quaderno no. 98: 11-22).

Giacomini, Valerio and Valerio Romani. 1982. *Uomini e parchi.* Milano: Angeli.

Graziani, Carlo Alberto. 1989. La tutela della natura e l'istituzione dei parchi nazionali: Erminio Sipari, l' "apostolo" del Parco nazionale d'Abruzzo. In Costantino Felice and Luigi Ponziani (eds.), *Intellettuali e società in Abruzzo tra le due guerre,* 127 et seq. Bulzoni: Rome.

Pedrotti, Franco (ed.). 1996. *I parchi nazionali nel pensiero di Renzo Videsott.* Camerino: Università degli Studi di Camerino.

—. 2007. *Il Parco nazionale del Gran Paradiso nelle lettere di Renzo Videsott.* Trento: Temi.

Piccioni Luigi (1999), *Il volto amato della Patria. Il primo movimento per la protezione della natura in Italia 1880-1934.* Camerino, Università degli studi di Camerino.

—. 2000. La natura come posta in gioco. La dialettica tutela ambientale-sviluppo turistico nella storia della "regione dei parchi". In Massimo Costantini and Costantino Felice (eds.), *Storia d'Italia. Le regioni dall'Unità a oggi. L'Abruzzo,* 921-1074. Turin: Einaudi.

—. 2010. *Primo di cordata. Renzo Videsott dal sesto grado alla protezione della natura.* Temi: Trento.

Sipari, Erminio. 1926. *Relazione del Presidente del Direttorio provvisorio dell'Ente Autonomo del Parco Nazionale d'Abruzzo alla Commissione*

Amministratrice dell'Ente stesso, nominata con Regio Decreto 25 marzo 1923. Tivoli: Maiella.

Tassi, Franco. 1983. La situazione in Italia dei parchi e delle riserve: la sfida del 10% per gli anni 80. In *Atti del Convegno Nazionale 'Strategia 80 per i parchi e le riserve d'Italia, Camerino, october 28-30, 1980*, 65-78. Camerino: Università degli Studi di Camerino.

THE ABRUZZO NATIONAL PARK AND NATURE PROTECTION IN ITALY: THE RECURRENCE OF A CENTRALITY

LUIGI PICCIONI

Landmarks in a troubled history

If we make a comparison with other European countries, we can observe that the history of Italian protected areas is a relatively early one. The first national parks were established in the early 1920s, when they already existed only in Sweden, Switzerland and Spain, while in Great Britain, France and West Germany this aim will be achieved later, between 1950 and 1970.

This precocity, however, was not the outcome of strategic choices of the ruling classes, of widespread sensitivity, of shared beliefs and commitments. Italian parks have always been the result, both at the moment of their establishment and after, of the generous efforts of restricted élites or–from the 1970s on–strong movements from below. They have never been established thanks to a spontaneous and conscious effort on the part of political parties and governments.

As a consequence of this the history of Italian protected areas has been marked by periods of impulse, periods of dramatic back-stepping and long periods of paralysis. This caused in different moments the need for the presence of pioneering and exemplary experiences and personalities, experiences and personalities able to best represent the perspectives of the whole reality of Italian protected areas. In an interesting testimony of a few years ago, the protectionist Maurilio Cipparone described his approach to the world of Italian protected areas–about forty years ago–as the discovery of a world almost as adventurous as that of American cowboy films, with their good and bad guys, dreams, betrayals, epic fights, horseback rides, happy endings and I think that he did not go too far from the truth. Looking at the issue form another slant–and agreeing with Bertolt Brecht's Galileo who affirms "Unhappy is the land that needs a hero"–we could perhaps say that the Italy of the protected areas has too often needed heroes.

It is undeniable, for example, that between 1944 and 1969 the passionate and visionary work of an isolated and often misunderstood giant like Renzo Videsott represented an indispensable landmark for the whole world of Italian protected areas, and rather he was the only Italian representative in the international world of protectionism and a recognised example of rigour and competence in the management of his park, the Gran Paradiso National Park. In 1967, when his permanence in office was threatened by numerous hostile forces within and outside the Park, a television program with both his admirers, like the young Fulco Pratesi, and his opponents, like the general director of Mountain and Forest Economy, Vitantonio Pizzigallo, consecrated "his" park as the only Italian protected area really worthy of this name and managed according to European standards. Videsott, the subject of a wide biography that I published a few years ago, not only saved during the hard times of the war the Gran Paradiso Park and favoured its return to a full autonomy, but also effectively supported the return to autonomy of the Abruzzo Park, struggled for the establishment of new national parks in the Eastern Alps, worked for a federation of all Italian protected areas and for years exposed the views and problems of these areas in international meetings. In short, he kept alive the parks' flame during years in which in Italy hardly anyone knew what was happening at the international level nor even what protected areas actually were.

Really different was the case of the great popular impulse thanks to which different recently-established regions created–from the mid-1970s– their own parks, substituting for many years the central State organs. This impulse had in fact an important weight on the institutional path which led, in 1991, to the issue of the Italian framework law on protected areas.

An extraordinary peculiarity of the Abruzzo National Park is that of playing, on more than one occasion, even after many decades, a leading or at least catalyst role in the Italian protected areas movement.

The Abruzzo National Park, landmark in more than one period

When I first approached nature protection, over forty years ago, there was a great interest for protected areas because in those years ecology was emerging and quickly becoming popular. Inserts in weekly colour magazines on the four "historical" national parks were often published: Gran Paradiso, Abruzzo, Stelvio and Circeo. Actually, there was another national park, recently established, that of Calabria, but it was an anomalous park and in the majority of cases it was not even taken into account.

Whoever was curious to know more discovered that not all historical parks were equal. In fact two of them had been established in the early 1920s and the remaining two, around the mid-1930s. The first two, the Gran Paradiso and the Abruzzo parks, were managed by an Authority, while the other two, by the Corpo forestale dello Stato (State Forestry Corps). It was equally easy to know that the Abruzzo Park had lived really troubled events in recent years and that the Circeo was an especially wretched park: small, with unfortunate outlines and the target of very serious and more or less undisputed attacks.

In short it can be said that, despite all the efforts made by the magazines to show that the existing national parks were all important and worthy of attention, it was clearly evident that the Gran Paradiso and the Abruzzo parks had, for different reasons, something more than the other two: for the way they were managed, their naturalistic interest but also, and maybe mainly, for their historical events. This perception was founded and today we can say that it was more correct than we thought then. Thus let us go through some passages of the Abruzzo Park history, which in the last twenty years has been the object of various studies.

A pioneering park: 1911-1933

At the end of 1922 the Abruzzo National Park, together with the Gran Paradiso Park, became the first protected areas established in Italy. This achievement is not fortuitous because from 1911 the upper Val di Sangro and the Graian Alps were the first Italian areas pointed out by naturalists as worthy of protection: both the naturalist Lino Vaccari, in his report to the Unione Zoologica Italiana (Italian Zoological Union) end-of-year meeting, and the zoologist Alessandro Ghigi, in his design of the game maps presented during the Vienna International Hunting Conference, pinpointed in fact some extraordinary concentrations of rare species of animals and proposed creating there the first Italian national parks.

In the following years the proposals for new parks increased, but soon after the war the movement to establish national parks in Italy focuses only on three candidatures: Gran Paradiso in the North, Abruzzo in the Centre and Sila in the South of the country. Each proposal has its own promoting group characterised by different motivations, approaches and ambitions, even if all of them support common events within the Italian Touring Club and the Federazione Pro Montibus et Silvis (Association for Mountains and Forests) with *Il giornale d'Italia forestale* as mouthpiece of the whole movement.

Thus between 1913 and 1922 the Abruzzo area is at the centre of the initiative for the establishment of the Italian national parks and it has to be recognised that the Rome-Abruzzo group leading the initiative is the most dynamic of Italy. The promoters of the Calabria park, in fact, are moved essentially by a tourist evaluation which soon will give way to different evaluations on the use of resources in the Sila plateau, while the perspective of the national park of the Graian Alps–which will later become the Gran Paradiso–emerges really only from 1919, to solve the problem of the abandonment of the old royal hunt reserve. Even if the promoting group of the Alpine park will soon be enhanced by great scientific prestige figures such as Lino Vaccari and Oreste Mattirolo and by prominent politicians like the future president Giorgio Anselmi, the Rome-Abruzzo core definitely remains the most long-lived and dynamic. This group is so determined that faced by a substantial paralysis of the parliamentary passage it decides between 1921 and 1922 to force the hand of Parliament and government establishing the Abruzzo National Park as a private institution.

Also for this reason some people insist on dating the official birth of the Abruzzo park to the private inauguration held in Pescasseroli in September 1922 instead of the publication of the establishing decree in the Official Journal the following January, thus fuelling an futile controversy with the Gran Paradiso about which one is the "first Italian park".

From 1923 to 1933 the first two "historical" parks live an especially happy period characterised by the management autonomy, administrative boards whose members were figures of great scientific and political stature, enthusiastic and expert directors, a management style which has nothing to envy from the best foreign reserves. In 1933, however, all competences about national parks are handed over to the Milizia forestale nazionale (National Forestry Militia), which inaugurates a centralist and bureaucratic administration destined to create important damage. The two national parks established soon after, the Circeo and the Stelvio, are born under the mark of this management style and even after World War II they will not enjoy the benefits of the autonomy which the Abruzzo and Gran Paradiso will be able to reconquer.

A park as a negative example: 1962-66

This return to autonomy, that is the re-establishment of the decentralised and democratic management authorities like in 1922 when they were created, will be a hard-won achievement in which Renzo and Paolo Videsott will play a propulsive role, but the effects in the Alpine park and in the Apennine one will be different.

In fact, in the Gran Paradiso Park the clever direction of Renzo Videsott will allow an effective unhooking from the Corpo forestale dello Stato and the return to a complete autonomy, which will start weakening in the early 1960s due to ever-strengthening local political pressures. The re-establishment of the Authority of the Abruzzo National Park will be conceived, on the other hand, as a compromise between the local administration and the top officials of the Corpo forestale dello Stato, a compromise that will allow the latter to hold a solid if not total control of the Authority.

So during the 1950s there is a diarchy which includes the Authority's director, the lawyer Francesco Saltarelli, who was one of the main promoters of the return to autonomy, and the presidents of the Authority coming from the bureaucratic Corpo forestale. Over the years this diarchy will become more and more unstable and conflictive because the Corpo forestale will demonstrate itself as very sensitive to pressures coming from both local and national political and entrepreneurial circles, which intend to transform the upper Val di Sangro in a vast land of construction investments. On the other hand, Francesco Saltarelli and some exponents of Pescasseroli's old ruling classes will try to enforce the fundamental mission of the Authority: a rigorous nature protection within the reserve borders. This will lead to increasingly harsh conflicts, which will remain latent during the 1950s but will explode from the end of the decade. The dismissal in 1964 of the director Saltarelli by the president, the forestry-official Tavanti Tommasi, later convicted for crimes related to unauthorised building, will be the climax of such conflicts but also the beginning of a radical change of direction.

In fact, the desperate and ever more explicit attempt of Saltarelli and the old Pescasseroli leadership to bar Roman and Neapolitan constructors' way triggers from the summer of 1962 a resounding national press campaign destined to last many years which can be considered one of the founding moments for the birth of the modern Italian environmentalist association movement and a widespread awareness of the significance and role of protected areas in Italy. Thanks to this vast press campaign the Abruzzo National Park becomes–even if involuntarily–the catalyst of the rebirth of Italian parks. Paradoxically, by becoming a negative example, it has a more important role of incitement and civic education than the Gran Paradiso Park, well-managed by Renzo Videsott.

Over the years, in fact press intervention is not limited to information and accusation but deploys an extraordinary practical efficacy. During 1964, when the construction speculation seems to be unstoppable and the members of Parliament linked to the Corpo forestale present a bill to reform the Park Authority which would mean the end of the protected area, the wind starts blowing in the opposite direction. The president Luigi Tavanti Tommasi is removed, the presidency is taken on by an older and experienced forestry officer, Giulio Sacchi, who looks with consternation at the river of accusations and protests which are transforming the Abruzzo reserve into an international case. Thus begins a process that within five years will lead to discarding plans to dismiss the Authority, the appointment of a new director and the achievement of a new management style.

As I have already mentioned, the weight of the press campaign begun in 1962 has gone beyond the narrow borders of the upper Val di Sangro and has involved a series of important changes in Italian environmentalism and the common awareness of the problems related to nature protection. Clearly this has been possible also for a particular historical conjuncture, characterised by the conclusion of the industrial modernisation process of the country, a relative loss of the centrality of the class struggle traditionally embodied by the conflict between the Christian Democracy and the Italian Communist Party and the slow entering of the American "spring of ecology" into Europe. However, the "Abruzzo National Park war" fought between 1962 and 1969 was so harsh and visible at a national level that it became a catalyst of all these tendencies.

Once more at the centre of nature protection in Italy: 1969-1991

1969 is a crucial year for this story because it is when, thanks to some, in part, fortuitous circumstances, a young member of the World Wildlife Fund Italy, Franco Tassi, is appointed director of the Park Authority, five years after Francesco Saltarelli's dismissal. Tassi will remain at the Abruzzo Park for more than thirty years, until he will be removed as well, in 2002, and even if the last period of his management was debated and even dramatic, his direction deeply marked the history of the Park, the upper Val di Sangro, the Italian protected areas and nature protection itself in Italy.

The reasons of this great influence and thus the renewed prestige of the Abruzzo Park are linked to six characteristics of Tassi's direction, especially evident in the period 1969-1991.

1. *The definitive defeat of the construction assault and the political parties' interference.* From 1969 on the old and new attempts to construct buildings and infrastructures disrespectful of the landscape and naturalistic integrity of the Park territory are regularly stopped and repelled, with a determination unknown by the previous administrations and the other Italian parks. This is made possible by recurring systematically to the Court, sometimes provoking harsh conflicts with local administrators and communities, but obtaining an unquestionable success and often involving positively the younger and more sensitive administrators. In the same way the reiterated manoeuvring of national and regional political exponents, aimed at putting the Authority under control for objectives different from the institutional ones, is defeated.

2. *The internal renewal.* With the arrival of Tassi and a new staff (in which Giuseppe Rossi the current president, then very young, appears) and with the active support of the WWF Italy the Park Authority changes completely. What for years has been a "little park", with few employees, a shy and limited action and an opaque image, soon becomes an equipped, dynamical, modern institution, able to involve journalists, scholars, politicians and Italian and foreign citizens, but above all able to effectively communicate itself, its mission and the great results achieved. In a few months, thanks also to the moral support of Renzo Videsott, the baton of the best organised and most attractive Italian national park passes from Gran Paradiso to Abruzzo. Considering that in 1969 in Italy there are only five national parks, three of them in bad condition, two provincial parks not yet working and a handful of very small state reserves, the Abruzzo Park becomes without difficulty the symbol of renewal–even if hindered– of the world of Italian protected areas.

3. *A management workshop.* Only those who visited Pescasseroli and the other towns of the Park in the 1970s and in the early 1980s can have today a true view of how much the Park Authority has been a unique forge of ideas in terms of management innovation. In this period scientific research is organised around an original research facility; supervision broadens and is rationalised; an organic regulation concerning a large number of matters is issued, often with innovative or little known solutions; a faunal policy of large-scale effort is started; solid relationships with similar foreign institutions are developed; a theoretical reflection on environmental conservation and the problems concerning the relationship between protected areas and local realities is encouraged; a pioneering work of incitement for the supply and demand of what only many years later will be defined as "sustainable tourism" is set up through a network of museums, local offices and cooperatives; a sophisticated and articulated

initiative is set up to give to the reserve a "corporate image"; a vivacious initiative is launched in the gadget and specialised and popular publishing field. If in 2012 all this seems obvious, the effect in 1975 was greatly different, when the majority of these things in Italy were for the most part unknown.

4. *A national and international projection.* This "new" park is the focus of attention of public opinion and national and foreign institutions; it is, thus, a very visible park. This is partly possible thanks to the heritage of the 1960s press campaign, but maybe also and above all thanks to an inexhaustible ability to create relationships, talk to the press and the publishing reality, work on the collective imagination, gather around itself energy and personalities, learn from the foreign examples and link to them permanently. The Abruzzo reserve gains during those years an international prestige that still resists today.

5. *An essential centre for the diffusion of parks' culture.* Before the mid-1960s, when the journalist Antonio Cederna and the WWF "young members" conquer a widespread national visibility, the only people who knew something about and tried to raise public awareness about protected areas' culture in Italy, were Renzo Videsott and the elder Alessandro Ghigi. Under Tassi's direction the Abruzzo National Park becomes a real national radiation centre of such a culture, working in close relationship with the WWF Italy, which is undergoing a rapid expansion in terms of membership and visibility. For many years this will be the main place of reference in Italy to know what parks are and do, the place where the majority of publications and films, which will contribute to build a national imagination of protected areas, are realised or, at least, planned.

6. *For a long time, the spearhead of the movement.* This extraordinary pedagogic impulse, however, is not an end in itself, but is part of a political effort–already begun in the mid-1960s–aimed at the creation of a widespread and well-organised national sparks system. This effort focuses on two strictly related actions: on the one hand, the "10% Challenge" officially launched during a famous conference held at the University of Camerino in 1980, that is the struggle to achieve the conservation of 10% of the national land; on the other hand, the struggle, already started a few years earlier, for the issue of a framework law on protected areas. Both struggles will be won in the early 1990s thanks to the support of a large number of subjects, some of them far from and even hostile to Tassi and the WWF, but for a good part of the 1970s and 1980s Pescasseroli, here, this place, is the most innovative and efficient stronghold of the whole action.

The Park Authority's archive, library and photographic archive, especially rich and complete reserves, store an extremely detailed memory of this dynamism and centrality and when the on-going cataloguing work is finished, they will certainly become essential instruments for the history of the Authority as well as Italian protected areas and national environmentalism of the 1970s and 1980s.

The darkening of Tassi's model

Those who know well all these events, know that the picture I have outlined until now is a partial one; those who ignore them can legitimately ask why such an extraordinary history ends with the removal of its main creator. Describing the national centrality of the Abruzzo National Park in the 1970s and 1980s, in fact, I underlined the lights but not the shadows. Shadows, however, were various and dark and involved a very harsh relationship with local communities and other sectors of Italian environmentalism; in particular, they were the main protagonists of the decline and end of the management model inaugurated by Tassi.

This dark side I think is grounded on three elements which were also the basis of the first period's success, elements, in short, that determined both the rise and following fall of Franco Tassi's experience. I do not believe it appropriate to dwell too much on this aspect, but it seems to me that the strength and at the same time the weakness of Tassi's thirty-year-long administration were determined by a very strict idea of environmental conservation, an idea according to which an absolute, enlightened "reason" exists, which must be supported mainly–not only but mainly–using an uncompromising strength given by laws; a personalistic and strongly centralizing view of management; and an hegemonic ambition that is transformed into an uncompromising claim, regardless of the fact that centrality can only be based on an authority gained day after day and recognised by the majority of interlocutors.

In the early 1990s, in the period of its maximum success, the Abruzzo National Park is still a landmark but it has to work in an unknown backdrop, populated by various new subjects, wishful of autonomy and the Park is unable to deal adequately with this backdrop. Probably the closure, that will initially lead to a gradual loss of prestige and then to convulsive management events and the financial disorder of the end of the decade which will end with Tassi's dismissal, begins here. It is early, considering the state of research, to attempt a plausible periodization, but it can be supposed that the creative impulse and the leading role of the Abruzzo National Park Authority in the universe of Italian protected areas end at the beginning of the 1990s due to internal inadequacy and not to external attacks.

The troubled following period, characterised by a possibly necessary silence lowered on Tassi's management has to be, however, overcome: it is no longer possible to put in parenthesis what the internal and external action of the Abruzzo National Park Authority represented between 1969 and 1990, because this action represents a fundamental piece of nature conservation history in Italy, and because its knowledge is fundamental to understand the features of the Italian protected areas and because–more simply but not banally–it would be impossible to understand why when writing the name of the main Italian national parks on the most used web search engine there are 469,000 results for the Abruzzo reserve, 300,000 for the Stelvio and far fewer (under 230,000 results) for all the other reserves. And similar results appear when doing the research in English.

A return of prestige?

In the world of Italian protected areas, which today is richer and more articulated than forty years ago but which is at the same time victim of an unknown and very deep crisis, it is impossible to think of re-proposing an Abruzzo Park centrality either like that inaugurated by Sipari and his collaborators or that led by Franco Tassi. Nor, fortunately, does a return to a "negative" centrality, like that of the 1960s, seem currently predictable.

The Abruzzo, Lazio and Molise National Park maintains an important historical legacy, a prestige that in recent years it has been able to patiently construct and some internal resources which can still make of it a national and international landmark. This conference, the celebration for the ninetieth anniversary of the Park's foundation which will be held in autumn, the organisation of the historical archive and other events in progress allow us to think that instead of the old centrality it is possible to establish an authoritativeness that can–as in other periods–do great good to the Italian protected areas system and, more in general, to nature conservation in our country.

Bibliography

Giancristofaro, Emiliano (ed.). 1998. *La lunga guerra per il Parco Nazionale d'Abruzzo.* Lanciano: Rivista Abruzzese.
Arnone Sipari, Lorenzo. 2011. Introduzione. In Lorenzo Arnone Sipari (ed.), *Scritti scelti di Erminio Sipari sul Parco Nazionale d'Abruzzo (1922-1933),* 11-41. Trento: Temi.

Ielardi, Giulio. 2007. *Uomini e lupi. Il cammino dei parchi italiani nel racconto dei protagonisti*. Pisa: Ets.

Piccioni, Luigi. 2000. La natura come posta in gioco. La dialettica tutela ambientale-sviluppo turistico nella storia della "regione dei parchi". In Massimo Costantini and Costantino Felice (eds.), *Storia d'Italia. Le regioni dall'Unità a oggi. L'Abruzzo*, 921-1074. Turin: Einaudi.

—. 2010. Les Abruzzes, "région des parcs". Coopération et consensus dans la naissance et le développement du plus important système italien d'espaces protégés. In Lionel Laslaz, Cristophe Gauchon, Mélanie Duval-Massaloux and Stéphane Héritier (eds.), *Espaces protégés, acceptation sociale et conflits environnementaux. Actes du colloque international 16, 17 et 18 septembre–Chambery, Le Bourget-du-Lac*, 79-88. Chambery: Laboratoire EDYTEM, ("Collection EDYTEM", vol. 10).

Sievert, James. 2000. *The Origins of Nature Conservation in Italy*. Bern: Peter Lang.

Sipari, Erminio. 1926. *Relazione del Presidente del Direttorio provvisorio dell'Ente Autonomo del Parco Nazionale d'Abruzzo alla Commissione Amministratrice dell'Ente stesso, nominata con Regio Decreto 25 marzo 1923*. Tivoli: Maiella.

CONTRIBUTORS

Lorenzo Arnone Sipari

Lorenzo Arnone Sipari (l_arnone_sipari@hotmail.com) graduated in Humanities at the University of Cassino, with whom he published essays concerning mainly the formation and the role of élites in Southern Italy between the eighteenth and nineteenth centuries. He has written various articles both on Benedetto Croce's background and the genesis and development of the Abruzzo National Park. On this matter, he has recently edited *Scritti scelti* (Trento 2011) by Erminio Sipari, creator and first president of the Abruzzo nature reserve.

Gianluigi Ceruti

Gianluigi Ceruti (gianluigi.ceruti@libero.it) is counsellor lawyer of Judiciary Superior organs and owner of a law office working in the Environmental and Urban development Law sector. He was national vice president of the association Italia Nostra from 1980 to 1990, member of Parliament during the Xth Parliamentary term (1987-1992), president of the Technical committee for protected natural areas from 1992 to 2003 (high consulting state organ for technical-scientific profiles) and council member of the Abruzzo, Lazio and Molise National Park (2001-2006). Winner of the Airone Award 1991 given by Giorgio Mondadori Publisher for his action in favour of parks, he is author of numerous writings on environment and editor of the fundamental work *Aree naturali protette: commentario alla legge n. 394/1991* (Milan 1993).

Alberto D'Orazio

Alberto D'Orazio (albertodorazio@hotmail.com) graduated in Law at the University "La Sapienza" of Rome. He developed his professional career within one of the most important Italian banks carrying out executive functions in the management and coordination in the field of credit to businesses. He was active in the political movement of the Upper Sangro in the early 1970s and in the cooperation actions of the zone. He was a volunteer counsellor at the anti-usury office of Rome City Council. He has been municipal counsellor at Villetta Barrea (L'Aquila) since 1999. He has been president of the Abruzzo, Lazio and Molise National Park Community since 2006.

Carlo Alberto Graziani

Carlo Alberto Graziani (graziani@unimc.it) teaches Principles of Private Law at the University of Siena. He was dean of the Faculty of Law at the University of Macerata, where he taught Private and Agricultural Law disciplines, and was director of the Agricultural Law Institute "A. De Feo". He is member of the board of scientific reviews and of the Club dei Giuristi dell'Ambiente. He was municipal counsellor at Villetta Barrea (L'Aquila), member of the European Parliament, president of the Sibillini Mountains National Park, member of the management board of Federparchi and the Federation of Nature and National Parks of Europe (Europarc) and president of Europarc-Italy. He has also written on protected area matters.

Corrado Guacci

Corrado Guacci (stofauna@gmail.com) graduates in Economics at the University of Bologna. From the end of 1970s he collaborates with the Abruzzo National Park in research on wolves and bears. From March 1988 to May 1990 he takes care of the "Mainarde project", fourth enlargement in the history of the Park, of which he becomes management board member from 1995 to 2000. Included in the official list of people suitable to develop the activity of park director, he is interested in the history of the relationship between man and fauna in particular wolves and bears. From 1995 to 2010 executive officer of the Molise Region, he is, among other things, Environmental authority and coordinator of the Technical committee for evaluation of environmental impact. In 2003 he realises the website www.storiadellafauna.it and in March 2011 creates the History of Fauna Society "Giuseppe Altobello", of which he is currently the president.

Henri Jaffeux

Henri Jaffeux (henri.jaffeux0799@orange.fr), after specialising in the ambit of nature protection, he has spent the majority of his career at the French Ministry of the Environment where he mainly looked after dossiers and projects concerning protected areas and the fauna and flora inventory. In particular he was responsible for the appointment of French sites to the Natura 2000 European network and presided over the experts committee of the Council of Europe in charge of creating the pan-European ecological network. He is member of the Group of Experts on European Diploma of Protected Areas. He created and directs the Association pour l'Histoire de la Protection de la Nature et de l'Environnement [http://www.ahpne.fr/].

Franco Pedrotti

Franco Pedrotti (franco.pedrotti@unicam.it) was full professor of Botany and Ecology at the University of Camerino, where today he is professor emeritus. President of the Società Botanica Italiana from 1982 to 1990, he is one of the deans of Italian environmentalism being an active member of associations since the early 1950s. He is director of the collections "L'uomo e l'ambiente" of the University of Camerino and "Natura e aree protette" of the publisher Temi of Trento and he established the postgraduate school in Management of natural environment and protected natural areas of the University of Camerino. In the last fifteen years he has published various monographs on nature protection and protected areas history in Italy, among these Il *fervore dei pochi. Il movimento protezionistico italiano dal 1943 al 1971* (Trento 1998), *Notizie storiche sul Parco Nazionale dello Stelvio* (Trento 2005) and *Notizie storiche sul Parco Adamello-Brenta* (Trento 2008).

Luigi Piccioni

Luigi Piccioni (l.piccioni@unical.it) received in 1999 his doctorate from the Scuola Normale Superiore di Pisa and presently he is research fellow at the University of Calabria. Among his publications the book *Il volto amato della patria. Sul primo movimento italiano per la tutela* della *natura 1883-1934* (Camerino 1999) and the essay "La natura come posta in gioco. La dialettica tutela ambientale-sviluppo turistico nella storia della 'regione dei parchi'", in the volume on Abruzzo of *Storia d'italia* Einaudi (Turin 2000).

James Sievert

James Sievert (james.sievert@cls-communication.com) received his doctorate in Modern European History at the University of California, Santa Cruz, and has held seminars and courses in American, Italian, Japanese and Chinese universities. Presently he lives in Aesch, Switzerland where he works as a professional translator. He is author of the book *The Origins of Nature Conservation in Italy* (Bern 2000).

François Walter

François Walter (Francois.Walter@unige.ch) teaches Modern and Contemporary History at the Faculty of Humanities at the University of Geneva. During his career he has studied, among other matters, the history of Switzerland, urban, landscape and environment and territory history. He has been visiting professor in universities and research centres of many countries among them the University of Freiburg, the Ecole Polytechnique

Fédérale of Zurich, the University Paris I Panthéon-Sorbonne, the Ecole des Hautes Études en Sciences Sociales, the Max Planck Institut für Geschichte of Göttingen and the Laval University in Québec. Among his works on environmental history *Les Suisses et l'environnement. Une histoire du rapport à la nature du XVIIIe siècle à nos jours* (Geneva 1990) and *Les figures paysagères de la nation. Territoire et paysage en Europe (16e-20e siècle)* (Paris 2004) have great relevance.

ILLUSTRATIONS

The Upper Sangro Valley: a pastoral vocation area.

Since the beginnings of the twentieth century "intensive logging".

The royal hunt reserve: a relation between the local notables and the Crown based on the bear hunting. Hunt with the Duke of Aosta (October 1921).

PARCO NAZIONALE D' ABRUZZO
Campo nazionale dell' A. S. C. I. a Fondillo (Opi) - 28 agosto 1921
IL QUADRATO DEI GIOVANI ESPLORATORI DURANTE IL DISCORSO INAUGURALE DI S. E. SIPARI

From the royal reserve to proposal for the National Park: the first jamboree in Val Fondillo to promote the project (August 1921).

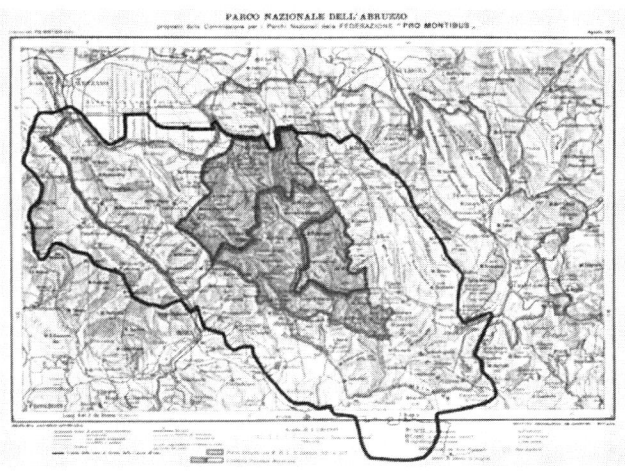

The 1917 first proposal for the borders of the Park.

The first symbol of the National Park Authority (1923)

The Park Authority officers in the early 1920s (seated from left the President
Erminio Sipari and the Director Nicola Tarolla).

The Park Rangers in the mid-1920s.

Touristic promotion activity: 1933 brochure in English by Park Authority-Italian railways (Ferrovie dello Stato)-National Tourist Office (Enit).

The symbol of the re-established Park Authority in early 1950s.

1960s, a park at risk: the killing of big mammals.

1960s, a park at risk: logging.

1960s, a park at risk: denounce on the important national press against the construction speculation.

Premonitory signs of the rebirth: European Diploma of Protected Areas (1967).

Premonitory signs of the rebirth-international interest: Philip of Edinburgh in
Pescasseroli guest of the WWF (1970).

ITALIA NOSTRA

PIANO DI RIASSETTO DEL PARCO NAZIONALE D'ABRUZZO
COORDINATORE : FULCO PRATESI_ L.BORTOLOTTI _ F.BRUNO _ P.CANNAVÒ_ V.GIACOMINI _
A.OSIO_ L.PIERUCCINI _ F.PRATESI_ G.ROSSI-CRESPI_A.M.SIMONETTA_F.STRINGHER_F.TASSI

The premonitory signs of the rebirth: Italia Nostra's plan for the Park (1968).

The new symbol of the Abruzzo National Park from the early 1970s and the campaign of the mid-1970s against the ski lift on the Marsican Mountain.

Demolition of the illegal construction complex of the Cicerana,
in the heart of the Park.

The rebirth of scientific research in the Park: "Saint Francis and the wolf"
campaign (1972).

The launch of education activity: the enlargement and renovation of the Visitor's Centre of Pescasseroli.

The launch of education activity: work and study camps for young people.

Atti
del Convegno Nazionale
Strategia 80 per i parchi e le riserve d'Italia
(Camerino, 28 - 30 ottobre 1980)

Cronaca e relazioni

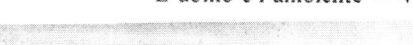
L'uomo e l'ambiente — 4

Camerino 1983

A leading role for the movement for the Italian protected areas: the launch of the
"10% Challenge" during the Camerino Conference of 1980.

Institutional prestige: the Minister for Environment Ripa di Meana visiting
Pescasseroli in early 1990s.

Institutional prestige: the President of the Republic Oscar Luigi Scalfaro during his
visit to Pescasseroli (1997).

The launch of the new millennium: the Abruzzo Lazio and Molise National Park hosts the Europarc meeting (2010).

An image of the conference of Pescasseroli in May 2012.

INDEX

Acerbo Giacomo, 35
Agostinone Emidio, 8, 9
Alberti Leandro, 31, 40
Alfonso II of Aragon, King of
    Naples, 33
Almagià Roberto, 14, 18, 19
Altobello Giuseppe, 14, 18, 19, 20,
    23, 34, 35, 36, 39, 40, 116
Amedeo of Aosta, Duke of Apulia,
    6, 35
André Gilbert, 69, 70
Anselmi Giorgio, 106
Antiphon, 81
Arnone Sipari Lorenzo, 1, 9, 19, 39,
    40, 100, 112
Baccarini Pasquale, 18
Balzano Vincenzo, 40
Bancel Nicolas, 60
Battaglia Felice, 81, 87
Bayer Ugo, 21
Beauquier Charles, 47, 63, 64, 65
Belprato Antonio, 33
Berlan-Darqué Martine, 71
Berlinguer Giovanni, 95
Bertarelli Claudio, 23
Bertarelli Luigi Vittorio, 24
Bétolaud Yves, 70
Blent Karin, 53, 60
Brecht Bertolt, 103
Bressou Clément, 67
Brunelli Gustavo, 19
Brunies Steivan, 56, 59
Bruno Giordano, 81
Burnat-Provins Marguerite, 49, 55
Camerano Lorenzo, 16
Cantelmo Restaino, 33
Caram Marguerite, 71
Carminati di Brambilla Giulio, 34
Catlin George, 85

Cederna Antonio, 90, 100, 110
Cederna Giuseppe, 100
Ceruti Gianluigi, 2
Chamson André, 68
Charles Felix, King of Naples, 33
Chouard Pierre, 67
Christ Hermann, 56
Cimini Nicola Vincenzo, 15, 21, 23
Cipparone Maurilio, 103
Coccia Francesco, 31
Coccia Leucio, 31
Colletta Pietro, 36
Conwentz Hugo, 50, 51, 52, 54, 55,
    60, 63
Corbino Orso Mario, 37
Corti Roberto, 22
Costantini Massimo, 100, 113
Couturier Marcel, 14, 68
Crema Camillo, 19
Critias, 81
Croce Benedetto, 5, 8, 9, 18, 28, 92,
    100
D'Andrea Uberto, 14, 36, 40
D'Orazio Alberto, 2
Daniel-Rops (Henri Petiot), 68
De Amicis Mansueto, 7
De Clermont Raoul, 47, 48, 60
De Lucia Vezio, 100
de Montenach Georges, 53
Debré Michel, 70
Di Pirro Giovanni, 11
Donzelli Giuseppe, 19
Dorotea Leonardo, 6, 11, 13, 14, 15
Duhamel Georges, 67, 68
Duke of Aosta, 120
Duke of Miranda, 36
Dumas Pierre, 70
Duval-Massaloux Mélanie, 113
Emerson Ralph Waldo, 54

Epicurus, 81
Fassò Guido, 81, 87
Felice Costantino, 40, 100, 113
Ferdinand I, King of Sicily, 36
Ferdinand IV, King of the Two
    Sicilies, 36
Ferrante I of Aragon, King of
    Naples, 33
Ferri Mauro, 23
Festa Enrico, 14, 35
Fiori Adriano, 18, 20
Fortier-Kriegel Anne, 71
Frigo Walter, 21
Galilei Galileo, 103
Gassot De Champigny L., 71
Gauchon Christophe, 113
Ghigi Alessandro, 13, 16, 19, 21,
    22, 23, 35, 94, 105, 110
Giacomini Valerio, 22, 94, 100
Giancristofaro Emiliano, 9, 40, 112
Giovannoni Gustavo, 18
Giron Charles, 47
Glutz Robert, 55, 61
Gortani Michele, 20
Grande Loreto, 12, 14, 20
Grant Ulysses, 85
Grassi Fausto, 97
Graziani Carlo Alberto, 1, 100
Groud Hervé, 53, 61
Gruvel Abel, 67
Guacci Corradino, 1, 23, 35, 40
Hall Ansel, 25
Hall Harvey M., 25, 28, 58
Harroy Jean-Paul, 71
Hazelius Artur, 53
Hedges Cornelius, 85
Heim Roger, 69, 71
Héritier Stéphane, 113
Hodler Ferdinand, 47
Hugo Victor, 67
Humbert Henri Jean, 67
Humboldt Alexander, 48
Ielardi Giulio, 113
Jaffeux Henri, 1, 71, 72
Kant Immanuel, 82
Keller Robert H., 28

Kozhevnikov Grigori
    Aleksandrovich, 60
Kupper Patrick, 56, 57, 58, 59, 61
Laborderie Baptiste, 38
Larissa-Basset Karine, 72
Larrère Raphael, 71
Laslaz Lionel, 113
Lavauden Louis, 67
Lenoir Marie Alexandre, 48
Leopold Aldo, 83, 87
Leporati Lamberto, 19
Lepri Giuseppe, 19, 35
Leynaud Emile, 72
Lizet Bernadette, 71
Löns Hermann, 53
Luigioni Paolo, 20
Mac Donald John, 84
Marsilius from Padua, 81
Martel Edouard-Albert, 65, 72
Mascilli Migliorini Luigi, 36, 40
Mathey Alphonse, 65, 66
Matschie Paul, 36
Mattirolo Oreste, 18, 106
Maure Marc, 53, 61
Mauz Isabelle, 72
Mels Tom, 58, 61
Merigonde Antoine, 38
Merveilleux du Vignaux François,
    70
Merveilleux Du Vignaux Pierre, 72
Miliani Giovan Battista, 18, 26, 28
Misiti Raffaello, 95
Monticelli Saverio, 16
Morris William, 82
Orano Paolo, 14
Orazi Antonio, 34
Pampanini Renato, 16, 18, 21, 23
Pantanelli Dante, 16
Paolucci Carlo, 13, 37, 38, 39
Parpagliolo Luigi, 18
Paruta Paolo, 81
Pedrotti Franco, 1, 40, 94, 100
Petit Georges, 67
Petrella Armando, 31
Petter Jean-Jacques, 71
Philip of Edinburgh, 126

Piccioni Luigi, 1, 9, 11, 19, 35, 40,
    45, 61, 89, 91, 94, 100, 113
Pirotta Pietro Romualdo, 12, 16, 17,
    18, 19, 20, 21, 23, 39, 40
Pizzigallo Vitantonio, 104
Polimanti Osvaldo, 19
Ponziani Luigi, 100
Pradelle Denis, 69
Pratesi Fulco, 90, 104
Prince of Naples, 7
Prioton Jean, 66
Quatremère de Quincy Antoine
    Chrysostome, 48
Regnault Henri, 82
Ricci Corrado, 8
Ripa di Meana Carlo, 132
Rivera Vincenzo, 19
Romani Valerio, 100
Roosevelt Franklin Delano, 84
Rossi Giuseppe, 96, 109
Rudorff Ernst, 47
Ruskin John, 82
Sabatier Michelle, 72
Sacchi Giulio, 108
Saltarelli Francesco, 21, 107, 108
Saltarelli Saverio, 93
Samivel (Paul Gayet-Tancrède), 68
Santi Flavio, 18
Sarasin Fritz, 56
Sarasin Paul, 55, 56, 58, 60, 61, 65
Sarti Ercole, 18
Scalfaro Oscar Luigi, 132
Schröter Carl, 55, 56, 58, 61
Sellars Richard West, 29
Selmi Adel, 72
Sérot Robert, 68, 69
Sievert James, 1, 9, 113
Sipari Carmelo, 7, 8, 11, 15, 34
Sipari Erminio, 6, 8, 9, 11, 14, 18,
    19, 20, 21, 23, 26, 27, 28, 29, 32,
    33, 34, 35, 36, 37, 38, 39, 40, 41,
    90, 91, 92, 95, 100, 112, 113,
    122

Sipari Family, 5, 7, 13
Sipari Francesco Saverio, 8, 11, 15,
    34
Sorrentino Annalisa, 9
Spallone Mario, 95
Spyri Johanna, 47
Tarolla Nestore, 11, 14
Tarolla Nicola, 11, 38, 122
Tassi Franco, 17, 20, 21, 28, 77, 90,
    93, 96, 97, 101, 108, 109, 110,
    111, 112
Tavanti Tommasi Luigi, 107, 108
Thibon Gustave, 68
Thomasius Christian, 81, 82
Thoreau Henry David, 54
Titta di Capua, 33
Togliatti Palmiro, 95
Tonzig Sergio, 22
Turek Michael F., 28
Umberto I, King of Italy, 7, 34
Ursitti Alessandro, 11
Vaccari Lino, 13, 14, 15, 18, 19, 20,
    21, 23, 26, 29, 39, 41, 105, 106
Varone Giuseppe, 9
Vayssière Paul, 67
Venturi Guido, 23
Videsott Paolo, 107
Videsott Renzo, 21, 22, 94, 95, 100,
    104, 107, 109, 110
Vincenti Pietro, 41
Vittorio Emanuele II, King of Italy,
    6, 15, 33, 34
Vittorio Emanuele III, King of Italy,
    7, 15, 34, 35
Walter François, 1, 46, 50, 52, 53,
    58, 61
Wettengel Michael, 52, 53, 61
Wilczek Ernest, 20
Wilson Edward O., 28
Wöbse Anna-Katharina, 59, 60, 61
Zschokke Friedrich, 56
Zwingli Ulrich, 81